Greene Acres Publications
PO Box 425
Honea Path, South Carolina
29654
United States of America

Printed in the United States of America on acid-free paper

First Edition ~ September 2005

Second Edition ~ April 2007
ISBN 1-932307-99-0

Design by Martha H. Greene
Graphics © 2005 Jupiter Images Corporation
Line Illustrations & Diagrams © 2005 by Martha H. Greene unless otherwise noted
Scripture quoted from the Holy Bible, King James Version

TREASURY
OF
VINTAGE
HOMEKEEPING
SKILLS

Collections of the Homekeeper

❧ Resources ❧
❧ Recipes ❧
❧ Records ❧

Written and Compiled
by:
Mrs. Martha Greene

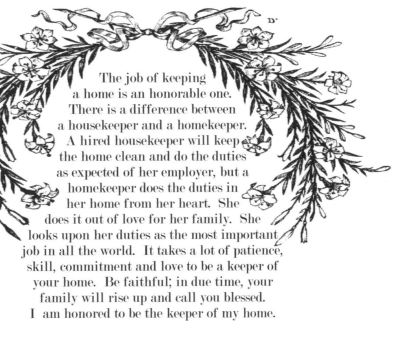

The job of keeping
a home is an honorable one.
There is a difference between
a housekeeper and a homekeeper.
A hired housekeeper will keep
the home clean and do the duties
as expected of her employer, but a
homekeeper does the duties in
her home from her heart. She
does it out of love for her family. She
looks upon her duties as the most important
job in all the world. It takes a lot of patience,
skill, commitment and love to be a keeper of
your home. Be faithful; in due time, your
family will rise up and call you blessed.
I am honored to be the keeper of my home.

Mrs. Martha Greene

Collections of the Homekeeper

This Treasury
Belongs to:

_____

_____

_____

Acknowledgements

Pages of this treasury are filled with
information shared by godly women, all keepers
of their homes, who were graciously willing to share
with us. I offer all of you my sincerest thanks and
have hope that the high calling of homekeeper
will in some small way be preserved
because of your generosity.

Martha Greene

Especially to:
Mrs. Rebekah Wilson
Mrs. Sharon Castlebury
Mrs. Marilyn Moll
Mrs. Lin Cazares
Mrs. Jan Stafford
Mrs. Kimberly Eddy
Mrs. Susan Vernon
Mrs. Lydia Sherman
Mrs. Laurie Latour
Mrs. Lydia Greene
Mrs. Gail Kappenman
Mrs. Kate Estes

"Make a home; beautify and adorn it; cultivate all heavenly charms within it; sing sweet songs of love in it; bear your portion of toil, and pain, and sorrow in it; con daily lessons of strength and patience there; shine like a star on the face of the darkest night over it, and tenderly rear the children it shall give you in it. High on a pinnacle, above all earthly grandeur, all gaudy glitter, all fancied ambitions, set the home interests. Feed the mind in it; feed the soul in it; strengthen the love, and charity, and truth, and all holy and good things within it!"

from ~ <u>The Royal Path of Life</u>, by Haines & Yaggy, 1879

❧ To ❧

Roger Alan Greene,

the husband of my youth.
It is an honor to be the keeper of your home.
I love you with all my heart.
Thank you for loving me.

Yours forever,

Martha

❧ Preface ❧

Several months ago, I read a post on an online discussion group. In the post, Lin Cazares was reminiscing about her grandmother's home-keeping notebook. Lin said, in part, *"My grandmother scheduled every facet of her housekeeping and considered it an actual occupation. . .it was her calling in life, and it showed in how meticulous she was with her notebook. It was a hard-bound book, about 5" x 8" and about an inch thick. She made detailed diagrams and sketches to illustrate her ideas. How I wish I had that notebook - I could learn a lot from her!"*

Instantly, my mind went back to my own grandmother's Depression-era kitchen. I have fond, vivid memories of walking into her kitchen, my youthful senses immediately awash in the tantalizing smells of spicy gingersnap cookies, homemade applesauce, and succulent blueberry pie. Imagine the glory of a childhood in which one awakens to the smell of baking blueberry muffins, waiting to be served hot for breakfast upon colorful, Fiestaware plates.

My friend, Martha Greene, read the same post by Lin Cazares. She was immediately inspired to create a vintage-flavored notebook on homekeeping skills – one that could be used by mothers today to pass on to their children. Martha consulted with me and other like-minded homekeepers, and she has compiled an incredibly useful and warm treasury of information for the homekeeper. *The Treasury of Vintage Homekeeping Skills* is truly a book whose time has come – again!

The Treasury represents a remarkable union of practical and useful information, thought-provoking and timeless quotations, delightful vintage graphics, and a wide variety of delicious recipes for all occasions. With the help of several contributors, the finished product covers such subjects as old-time medicinal home remedies, patterns for handiwork, outlines and ideas for gardening, instruction on baking and cooking, and a section on home business.

The Treasury of Vintage Homekeeping Skills is a loving and practical way for mothers today to pass on their homekeeping skills to their daughters and granddaughters. It encourages us to press on in the honorable profession of homemaking. This book deserves a place in every hope chest; a space on each woman's shelf who truly has a heart's desire to be a wife and mother. It is a work deserving of being preserved and passed on for many, many years to come.

Mrs. Marilyn Moll

Urban Homemaker ~ PO Box 72 ~ Paonia, Colorado 81428

Table of Contents

Homekeeping

Use this blank page for journaling or attach snippets and clippings for keepsakes.

" Housework is something I do that
nobody notices . . . . . unless I don't do it ! "

Use this blank page for journaling or attach snippets and clippings for keepsakes.

Cleaning

My grandmother showed me her public highschool home economics journal from the 1920's. It was very complete with notes on scheduling housekeeping skills and recipes. She had made an entire handwritten book on every imaginable facet of housekeeping. The really interesting thing is that she had the cleanest house that I have ever seen -- even the deep dark closets and corners. She also scheduled every facet of her housekeeping and considered it an actual occupation, just as my grandfather went out to go to his job each day. She never thought of it as a chore. This was her calling in life, and it showed with how meticulous she was with her notebook. It was a hard-bound book, about 5"x 8" and about an inch thick. Her writing was small and detailed. She made diagrams and sketches to illustrate her ideas. She even had a sewing section with sketches of each stitch and diagrams of various dress designs. How I wish I had that notebook! I could learn a lot from her.

Mrs. Lin Cazares

Most of us would like to be more successful at keeping a picture perfect home. Many times our lives get consumed with stressful situations, important projects, births of new babies, deaths of loved ones, and the house becomes disordered. You need to have a cleaning schedule but don't become a slave to it. We want a clean home for our families and guests, but it won't always be just as we would like it to be.

Work daily developing good habits to keep a clean home. Try to keep clutter to a minimum by putting scattered belongings in their proper places. Your home will appear in order even if you still have a long list of undone cleaning tasks. It is much easier to clean the home when things are picked up and put away. Schedule specific tasks for each day and more detailed cleaning tasks for each month and some tasks for twice a year.

Remember in all to enjoy your family and employ your children as handy helpers. The tasks will get finished, sooner or later. Before you know it, you will find the house is empty and you will wish for some little hands to get grubby fingerprints on your walls. Don't miss the moments by letting housework consume you. People are eternal beings, houses are temporal.

❧ Daily Cleaning ❧

List your daily tasks here.

_____

_____

_____

_____

_____

_____

_____

_____

_____

_____

_____

_____

_____

_____

Daily tasks look like this for a family with children. Each homekeeper's day will be different for her own situation and family size.

√ Bathrooms tidied and disinfected
√ Laundry maintained
√ Vacuum carpets
√ Straighten and put things in their places
√ Meals and dishes
√ Sweep floors and porches

.... Day by Day a Week Goes Round. ......

List an extra task for each day that will help keep your home spit-spot!

✖✖Monday✖✖

✖✖Tuesday✖✖

✖✖Wednesday✖✖

✖✖Thursday✖✖

✖✖Friday✖✖

✖✖Saturday✖✖

Add a task or two to your regular duties each day. Break up tasks throughout the week. Don't try to do it all in one day! Some tasks are:

Clean fingerprints from walls
Clean bathtubs
Mop and shine floors
Dust and polish the furniture

Wipe out and clean the refrigerator
Shake or wash throw rugs
Wipe down cabinets and doors
Change bedding & clean under beds

.......Week by Week a Month Goes Round.......

_____

_____

_____

_____

_____

_____

_____

_____

_____

_____

_____

_____

_____

_____

_____

Don't focus on what you didn't get done! Rejoice in what you did accomplish, even the small tasks! The "small things" add up to a cleaner home and a happier family.

Choose one day a month to add a few tasks to your regular duties that will keep your home clean and shiny.

Some tasks that need to be done monthly:

Vacuum furniture and flip cushions

Brush cobwebs from corners

Wipe down doors, knobs & switch plates

Dust blinds

Spot clean carpets

Wash ceiling fans

8

Spring Cleaning

"The chief aim of house-cleaning is to produce a sanitary condition and to make the home ready for the bright spring days. March is a busy month for the homemaker; there is a garden to plan, the spring outfits to sew, and standing out above and beyond everything else, the house to clean. Modern devices have so systematized the cleaning department of the home that the annual upheaval from attic to cellar has been partially eliminated. With all the rooms used during the winter they are given a weekly or daily cleaning. But there comes a time in the spring for the more thorough investigation of the closets and cupboards. One never realizes how fast the clippings and papers and magazines put aside to be read at our leisure can accumulate until our attention is called to them when cleaning day comes. During the early days of March with its variable weather, high winds and dark days, there will be an occasional sunshiny, warm day that brings out the dust streaks on the windows and the smoke-covered wallpaper becomes very noticeable. Then the housekeeper feels the need of indulging in the thorough renovation of the house. On all sides come the swish of the broom and the hum of the vacuum cleaner, the sound of the carpet beater and the backyard fills with lines of bedding and clothing showing that the campaign is on." from "The Young Housewife" ~1927

Do you groan at the thought of spring cleaning? Rejoice that you probably don't have smoke-covered wallpaper or have the task of hanging heavy carpets on the line, beating them with a carpet beater! These days, we have every convenience and an abundance of cleaning products to make our housecleaning tasks much easier than in grandmother's day. Think of spring cleaning as "detailing" the home. You've seen places that detail cars — they buff out scratches, wax the car, clean the upholstery and tend to many details that aren't normally done on a regular basis when the car is washed. It is the same thing with spring cleaning. "Detail" your home and attend to many things that don't get done during your normal cleaning routines. The tasks that need to be done vary from home to home but the goal is the same as it was in 1927: "The chief aim of house-cleaning is to produce a sanitary condition and to make the home ready for bright spring days." Not only do we want to live in a clean and sanitary home but we also need to bring order to our living area so that we can find things we need and so that our homes are a peaceful and orderly refuge for our families. ∿ *Mrs. Laurie Latour*

Homemade Cleaners

The products available in today's stores and markets for cleaning your home give you more choices than your grandmother could have ever imagined! Years ago, the homekeeper made her own from ordinary household products. Admittedly, there are many cleansers manufactured today that work more efficiently than the homemade cleaners of yesteryear, but it must be considered that many of these modern concoctions made by large factories are very caustic and harmful to our family's health. You may choose to try some of these easy-to-make household cleaning products and be very satisfied with the results.

Cleanser for Heavily Soiled Hands

Save all odds and ends of bar soap of every description. When enough has accumulated, break into small pieces and put through the food grater, using the medium cutter first, and then the fine cutter. To one cupful of this granulated soap add one and one-half cupfuls of cornmeal and put through the food chopper once again until reduced to a coarse meal. This may be facilitated by rubbing between the hands to loosen the particles. When all will pass readily through a meal sieve, add two tablespoons of olive oil to each two and one-half cupfuls of the soap and cornmeal mixture. Blend thoroughly. An ordinary fruit jar, with the rubber ring in place, makes a good container. A quantity of this cleanser kept on the kitchen sink or in the wash room will be found invaluable for cleansing very soiled hands and keeping them soft and smooth. It is perfectly harmless and costs next to nothing.

Washroom Discoveries

from
Good Housekeeping's Book of Menus, Recipes and Household Discoveries
~ Tenth Edition, 1925 ~

Spot ~ Stain Pre-treatment
½ cup white vinegar
½ cup water
½ cup liquid laundry detergent
½ cup ammonia
Mix together and put in a squirt bottle. Use on dirty collars, grease spots, and stains. Treat stain and launder as usual.

Stubborn Stain Soak
½ cup dishwasher powder
½ cup color~safe bleach
2 gallons very HOT water
Mix in a pail and add in clothing spotted with stubborn stains. Let soak overnight and then launder as usual. This works well on stained baby clothes.

Gossip is like mud on white socks . . . You can wash it off, but it leaves a stain!

Spray Disinfectant Cleaner

A marvelous easy-to-make homemade cleaner that kills mold and disinfects surfaces. Wonderful on kitchen counters!

 1 ½ tsp. borax
 2 Tbsp. white vinegar
 2 ¼ cups hot water
 ¼ tsp. eucalyptus essential oil
 ¼ tsp. lavender essential oil
 3 drops tea tree oil

Mix all together and stir until dry borax is dissolved. Pour into an empty spray bottle. Spray as needed on surfaces, wipe down and scrub on stubborn spots. Then rinse with a clean, damp cloth.

Resources
Frontier Herbs   ~   essential oils and tea tree oil   ~   800.669.3275
Phoebe Rose Soaps   ~   essential oils and empty bottles   ~   864.303.5113

Homemade Handy Wipes

You will need between 2 and 4 cups of cleaning solution, depending on the size and absorbency of the paper towel product selected. This recipe makes about 3 cups of solution.

General Surface Cleaning:

 1 ½ cups white vinegar
 1 ½ cups water

Place the lid on the plastic food storage container, and allow paper towels to absorb the cleaning solution for at least 4 hours. Open the food storage container. Gently pull out the wet cardboard tube from the center of the paper roll and discard. Carefully pull the end of the paper towels from the inside where the cardboard roll had been. Pull gently on the exposed end. Tips: As you use the wipes, they will begin to dry out, so add more water or cleaning solution as necessary. Allow the wipes to stand overnight before continuing to use them after adding more solution. Less solution and more water makes for a milder cleaning product.

~ *Mrs. Lorrie Flem*

Beauty on a Budget, Homemade Household Helps for a Beautiful Home
Used with permission
Mrs. Lorrie Flem ~ TEACH Magazine ~
18016 West Spring Lake Drive, Renton, Washington 98058

Receipts for Homemade Cleaners

In the 1800's, recipes were commonly called "receipts." Webster's New World Dictionary of the American Language acknowledges "receipt" as an old-fashioned variation of the word "recipe." Record your favorite "receipts" for homemade cleansers you have discovered.
When your daughters begin their own homes they will want the receipt for Momma's Favorite Cleanser.

More Receipts for Homemade Cleaners

Clothes Detergent

Put these ingredients in a large, old saucepan and heat until dissolved:

    1 bar of Ivory™ bar soap, cut in chunks

    1/2 cup powdered clothes detergent containing baking soda

    1/2 cup borax

    6 cups water

Pour this mixture into a 2-gallon container and fill up with hot water to make 2 gallons of mixture. Add in 1 tsp. of essential or fragrance oils for scented detergent, if desired. Stir with a large wooden spoon and place lid on snugly. Let stand and set up overnight. Ready to use for washing clothing. Will not be a heavy sudsing action but will clean clothes nicely. Use 1 cup of white vinegar for final rinse water, if desired.

Detergent for an Automatic Dishwasher

Mix and put into a labeled container:

    2 cups baking soda

    2 cups borax

Fill soap pocket with dish detergent powder and fill rinse pocket with white vinegar. Inexpensive and reliable.

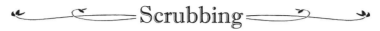
Scrubbing

Ovens

Cleaning the oven is important, as drippings or spills can cause the oven to catch fire. Scrubbing the oven is easier if you first lift off the oven door. Certainly a homemade cleaner will not be as potent as an industrial strength oven cleaner, so take heed. Wiping up spills and drips as they occur will be much easier to clean up than after they have baked and re-baked! Line the bottom of a clean oven with aluminum foil and it won't be necessary to scrub the oven as often. Just lift the foil and discard it with all the drips and mess and replace it after you have wiped down the inside of the oven. For a non-toxic oven cleaner, use a spray bottle to spray the bottom of the oven with hot water. Pour baking soda over it thickly. Allow to stand for 30 minutes and then spray with white vinegar, which will make a foaming action. Let stand a few minutes and then use a metal spatula to scrape off and remove baked on food, grease, and soda mixture. Use a scrubbing brush, steel wool scrubbing pads, and hot water and scrub off any residues. Wipe with a clean, wet cloth. Line with clean foil. Be sure to give the area under the oven a good cleaning at least twice a year. Have a strong fellow help in removing it. If you have a bottom storage drawer under your oven, it is easily removed and you have free access to clean under the oven. To clean top burner plates: Place them in a large pot of water (enough to cover), and add in 3 tablespoons powdered dishwashing detergent. Boil 15 minutes. Remove and clean off debris and dirt with a scrubby brush. Rinse, dry and replace.

Windows

Locate a 1-gallon container with a secure cap. Add in 1 pint rubbing alcohol, 4 tablespoons ammonia, 1 drop blue food coloring (helps identify the liquid as a cleaning agent), and 1 tablespoon of liquid soap. Fill the remainder of the gallon container with warm water. Shake and store for cleaning glass and windows. Use a lint-free cloth or paper toweling to clean your windows and glass. A squeegee makes the job a cinch! You can touch up the corners with your cloth if using the squeegee. Only a small amount of cleaner is needed. Empty spray mist bottles are readily available to keep an amount of window cleaner handy.

Homemade Shoe Scrubber

Take an 8" square of wood and attach two wooden scrubbing brushes, bristles up, onto the block of wood. Attach the brushes with screws, about 4 to 6 inches apart. Before entering the home, run your shoes over and between the brushes to remove any mud. This will save many minutes of scrubbing muddy spots on carpets and floors at the back door entrance.

Refrigerators

Refrigerators need to be wiped down weekly with a damp, soapy cloth to remove fingerprints and smudges. Each month, remove all the contents of the refrigerator and wipe down the inside. Use a large bowl of warm, soapy water containing ¼ cup of white vinegar. After cleaning, dry out the inside with an absorbent, dry cloth. Wipe down any jars or food containers if needed. Discard any spoiled foods. Twice a year, pull out refrigerator and scrub and clean under it. Remove dust from the back of the refrigerator coils with a vacuum or small dustbroom. Consult your owner's manual to locate coils and follow the manual's advice on cleaning them. This will prolong the lifespan of your refrigerator and make it run more efficiently. Keeping an open container of baking soda or a few pieces of charcoal in the back of the refrigerator helps to eliminate odors. What a pleasure to open a fresh, clean, cold refrigerator!

Sinks & Bathtubs

Record here your favorite cleansers and methods for cleaning these items:

_____

_____

_____

_____

_____

_____

_____

_____

_____

_____

_____

_____

_____

_____

This is the way we scrub the tub. . .scrub the tub. . .scrub the tub!
This is the way we scrub the tub on a Saturday morning.

A nice touch a loving wife can add to the master bed is hand-embroidered sheets. In years gone by, a young lady would carefully prepare the bedding she packed away into her hope chest in anticipation for the bridal bed. No pains were spared as she carefully embroidered the top sheets and pillowcases. The sheets were carefully hemmed and the pillowcases stitched together with perfect French seams.

Today, a homemaker can add this very old-fashioned touch. She will first need to invest in quality 100% cotton sheets. They are preferred because they can be taken from the washing machine and hung on the line to dry. They will be crisp and as fresh as the outdoors. If you fold them twice before hanging, (the way you would unfold them on the bed), they will not take up as much room on the clothesline. Embroider across the top of the flat sheet or place a simple little motif right in the corner of the band. Don't forget to embroider the end bands on your pillowcases to match the pattern on the sheet. Do iron your pillowcases; they will be so nice!

❧ Mrs. Sharon Castlebury

"Marriage is honorable in all and the bed undefiled."
~ Hebrews 13:4

In the holy bonds of matrimony the bed is pure, clean, and blessed. How is your bed? Have you possibly defiled it with your negligence or insensitivity? Is your bed clean? Who considers it a pleasure to climb into a rumpled, messy lump of bed coverings? Wash your sheets and smooth the wrinkles with care. Show your beloved he is still your true love. Air your pillows and cover them with lovely silk and cotton covers. Dust and polish the bed stands and add a small bud vase of flowers. Bestow on the one who holds your heart special favors of kindness and you will be blessed.

How to Make a Bed

The following directions should be followed by those who do this task. Put on the under sheet, so that the wrong side of the sheet shall go next to the bed, and the marking come at the head, tucking in all around. (This applies to those using a set of flat sheets instead of a fitted bottom sheet.) Then put on the pillow covers, even, so that the open ends shall come to the sides of the bed, and then spread on the upper sheet, so that the wrong side shall be next to the blankets, and the marked end at the head. This arrangement of sheets is to prevent the part where the feet lie from being reversed so as to come to the face, and also to prevent the parts soiled by the body from coming to the bed tick and blankets. Then put on the other coverings, except the outer, and tucking in all around, and then turn over the upper sheet, at the head, so as to show a part of the pillows. When the cases of the pillows are clean and smooth, they look best outside of the cover, but not otherwise. Then draw the hand along the side of the pillows, to make an even indentation, when the covering is pulled over them, and then smooth and shape the outside covering over the pillows. A careful homekeeper always gives attention to the manner in which a bed is made, but in some parts of the country it is rare to see this task performed in this proper manner.

Adapted from Treatise on Domestic Economy
by Catharine E. Beecher, 1841, Boston

⧫⧫⧫⧫⧫ Mattress Sizes ⧫⧫⧫⧫⧫

Standard King: W=78" x L=80"
California King: W=72" x L=84"
Queen: W=60" x L=80"
Double or Full: W=54" x L=75"
Twin or Single: W=39" x L=75"
Crib: W=28" x L=52"
⧫⧫

Standard sizes ~ Some manufacturer's mattress sizes may vary.

❧ Linen Spray ❧

It is very simple to make some lovely scented mist with which to spray your bedding linens while making up your bed. Take 4 oz. of Rose Water. Drop in 8 drops of Ylang-Ylang essential oil and 6 drops of lavender essential oil. Replace lid and shake to combine. Pour into a small spray mist bottle. Label with a pretty homemade label. Spray your bedding linens liberally while making your bed. When you turn back the sheets, a soft, pleasant fragrance will waft through the air.

Rose Water available from Frontier Herbs 800.669.3275 Small empty spray mist bottles available from Variety or Discount stores. Check the cosmetic departments.

Linen Spray makes a lovely bridal gift with a set of embroidered pillowcases.

Vintage Embroidery Pattern
for
~ Sheets & Pillowcases ~

Copied with permission from <u>Needlework Skills Book 1</u> by Rebekah Wilson
For more vintage patterns and embroidery guides write to:
Rebekah Wilson
Hope Chest Legacy
PO Box 1398 Littlerock, CA 93543
~ (888.554.7292) ~

Sewing Your Own Bed Sheets

Use soft, fine thread count cotton fabrics. To make sheets larger than crib or twin size you will need to use wide-width fabrics such as un-bleached muslins or add a width of fabric (join with French seams) on each side to make the fabric wide enough. Wash and dry your fabrics.

~ Fitted Sheet ~

Take your top mattress measurement. Add the depth of the mattress to this measurement on each side and the ends. Draw a square template on a piece of stiff paper that has the measurement of the depth of your mattress + 2" added to that measurement. (i.e., If your mattress depth is 8" then make a square template that is 10".) Lay this even with each corner edge and cut out this square area from each corner. (You will only be cutting on two sides of the square.) Match wrong sides of cuts together and sew up the seam with a scant seam and then turn to right sides to gether and sew up seam again with a ¼" seam. This makes a French seam and a nice ravel free finish. Hem all around the sheet by folding up ¼" and then folding up again to hide the raw edge. Finish off your fitted bed sheet by stretching and stitching a 10" length of ½" wide elastic at each corner. Fold elastic length in half and place on corner seam line; stretch and stitch to one end and then start back at the middle and stretch and stitch to opposite end, stretching while stitching down.

~ Flat Sheet ~

This will be simple as it is only a flat piece of fabric hemmed on all 4 edges. For the top edge of the sheet use a 3"-4" hem for a nice border. Embellish with embroidery, flat lace, or ribbon if desired.

~ Finished Sizes of Flat Sheets ~

Crib: W=42" x L=72"
Twin or Single: W=66" x L=96"
Full or Double: W=81" x L=96"
Queen: W=90" x L=102"
Standard King: W=106" x L=108"
California King: W=102" x L=110"

This allows for about 8"+ to tuck in at the foot of the bed.

Pillowcases

Cut fabric to match your bed sheets, 40" x 33". If making queen or king cases you will need to add more length since the pillows made for larger beds are longer in length. Fold in half so rectangle measures 20"x 33". Sew up 20" side (opposite to fold edge) and across one end with a narrow seam. Finish off the seam. If you do not have a serger to make a nice ravel-free finish, then sew the seam with wrong sides together with a scant seam. Turn and press and sew again with a ½" seam with right sides together. This forms a French seam. Turn down the open end of the case ½" and press. Then turn down again 4" and press. Stitch down close to the folded edge. Add an embroidered embellishment, or a piece of satin ribbon, or flat lace stitched over the stitched line.

Vintage Embroidery Design

~ for embellishing pillowcases ~

Laundry

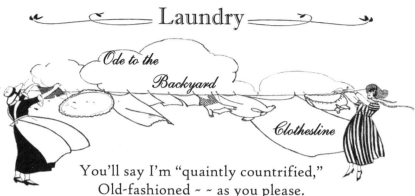

Ode to the Backyard Clothesline

You'll say I'm "quaintly countrified,"
Old-fashioned ~ ~ as you please.
But I love the sight of fresh, clean laundry
Tossing in the breeze.
To suspend each garment on the line,
Then give the wind full play;
To caress and gently fragrance
In that sweet "outdoorsy" way.
They bask in sunny radiance,
Towels neatly hung in rows;
Snowy linens snapping crisply,
Darling dancing baby clothes.
And when at dusk I gather them
I feel extremely blessed
That line-dried and sun-kissed cleanliness
Clothes the ones that I love best.

by: *Juanita M. Vernon*

The Laundry Room

Keep it clean and orderly. Decorate it cheerfully so that it won't be a trial for you to get in there and do your work. Use wall borders and accessories that help you enjoy having a laundry room. Keep the dryer and washer free from clutter on the tops. Hang shelves for your supplies and detergents. Have respect for yourself and treat your clothes with thankfulness and love. Your family is special. Each one deserves to have clothing which fits properly and has not been treated horribly by shoving all the colors and textures into one large load. All your family's clothes should be able to have the label ~

Washed with
tender loving care

Do not overstuff your washing machine. Leave room for the water to circulate and clean your soiled clothes. Be gentle with your machine — it works for you, so you do not have to boil and stir clothes over a hot fire like great-granny!

22

Before you wash the laundry, soiled clothing should be sorted into piles. Separate piles into baby clothes, towels, jeans, etc. Some garments need to be washed on the delicate cycle. The normal cycle wrings out the water at a very fast spin. This can ruin delicate items.

Jeans & Overalls :

Blue jeans and denims bleed blue into the water. Unless you want your white socks and underwear light blue or your prize tablecloth slightly blackened, wash jeans separately or with other blues or similar types of fabrics. Don't throw in a blue dress, unless the blue dress is of a sturdy fabric like the jeans. Just because the garment is the same color does not mean you wash it in the same load.

White Underwear :

Tee-shirts, socks, and other underclothing made of sturdy cotton can be washed in hot water on the normal cycle, then dried in the dryer on a hot setting. Remember, not all whites can be washed this way. Some whites, such as delicate women's clothing or things like doilies, table runners, and laces, must be hand-washed and treated carefully.

Towels :

Make two piles of dirty towels on your laundry room floor, or have baskets for each kind of laundry. One pile is white and pastel, and the other is dark. Some find it advantageous to purchase only white bath towels because it is easier to wash them. However, dark colored towels are desirable for other reasons. Whatever the case, sort them into two wash loads and do not wash them together. If you do, you will find the light ones become muddied in color, and the dark ones will lose their color and fade, lacking their fresh, new look.

Dish Towels :

These should always be washed together, separate from clothing, and preferably in hot water. It would be a good idea to put them in a separate basket to collect them for washing rather than in the general laundry basket. They need a disinfectant or bleach to sanitize them. Potholders can be treated in the same way and need to be washed on a regular basis as they collect debris on them. Placemats and table-cloths should be washed separately from dishtowels on a gentler cycle. Do not use hot water on them as they will fade.

Bedding : If the bedspread or comforter is mostly for decoration, it isn't necessary to wash it except during spring cleaning. Excessive washings will wear it out unnecessarily. If you have a bed set with matching curtains and accessories, you may be disappointed if the spread fades in comparison to the other accessories due to excessive washing. To save wear and tear on a matching spread, take it off the bed before sleeping and place it on a quilt rack or the back of a chair. If you choose to wash it often, you will need to wash the other accessories and curtains at the same time so they will wear and fade at the same pace. Blankets also do not need to be washed all the time — maybe twice a year if there has been no sickness or stains spilled on them. (If you want to freshen them, they can be hung over the clothesline in the fresh air for a while.) Fresh bed sheets are used to help protect the blankets from odors and soiling. Wash sheets as often as you like, following the same rules for washing towels.

Outerwear : Check the labels on garments and sort them into piles according to washing instructions. Not all clothes that require cold water should be put together because some will fade and some require a different kind of spin cycle. Sort these further into piles according to color and type of cycle. The normal cycle will generally be rougher on the garment than the delicate cycle. Nylons, women's garments, and baby clothes do well on the gentle cycle. Remember to wash white blouses and shirts separately.

Blankets, rugs and car seat covers : Don't wash these with any other clothing or linens, but don't wash them all in the same load either. You'll have a terrible mess on your hands, as a washable rug gets soil and all kinds of things on the car seat cover that will be impossible to remove, and the blankets will not get clean. Wash each of these things separately. You may need to run a plain, clean water rinse with a little white vinegar or even bleach after washing particularly dirty items before you do another load of regular clothing.

Nylons and small things : Baby socks and other things that seem to lose their mates in the wash can be corralled inside a mesh bag. Look for these in discount stores. If you have trouble with socks that go missing in the washing machine, this will solve your problem and make sorting and folding clean laundry much less tedious.

ℛ *Mrs. Lydia Sherman*

~ Used with permission from Lady Lydia ~
~ Ladies Against Feminism ~

Mother's Clothespin Bag

½ yard cotton durable fabric
1 wire garment hanger
bias cotton binding tape

Take a wire garment hanger and lay it on ½ yard of fabric that has been folded. Fabric will measure approximately 18x22 inches when folded. Hanger will be bent in direction of arrow later.

Lay hanger on the fabric and trace around top curve of wire hanger with a piece of chalk.

Cut 2 pieces out following this top curve line that measure about 12-14 inches in length. See illustration for shape to cut. Trim out a small curve around back piece where neck of hanger will be.

Cut out an oval on middle front piece. See illustration. Oval is 6 inches long. This is the opening to reach in and retrieve your clothespins. Trim and buttons may be stitched on the front piece for an extra special touch. See illustration.

Sew FRONT & BACK pieces together, with right sides together, using a ½ inch seam. Sew around all 4 sides, leaving oval area open. Finish off seams with a zigzag stitch, overlock serger or encase in bias seam tape for extra durability.

Encase oval area in bias seam tape. Press all seams with a steam iron for a crisp look. Bend wire hanger as shown in illustration and insert into clothespin bag. Fill with clothespins. Hangs conveniently on the clothesline to access your clothespins while hanging laundry on the line. Store clothespin bag inside laundry room for protection from weather.

25

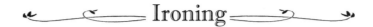

Ironing

"This is the way we iron our clothes, iron our clothes, iron our clothes! This is the way we iron our clothes, on a Friday morning."

I have memories of turning back the chenille spread on the full-size bed in my Grandmother's house. It was a cozy two-bedroom home with every room in impeccable order. The yard matched the neatness of the inside and was smiling with neat flower beds that were brimming with periwinkles. One room belonged to PaPa and MaMa and the other was the spare room. This spare room was my place to stay when I visited MaMa. I always knew what awaited me when I turned down the spread to crawl into that bed—pillowcases on fluffy pillows that smelled of the fresh outdoor air. They were always perfectly pressed and had the crease marks where she had pressed them into a neat square. Fresh pillowcases could be found stacked in perfect order in the linen cupboard. The sheets were just as smooth and made of fine count cotton thread with years of wear and yet snowy white.

I will confess, I cannot match the dedication she had to her home duties. I will be the first to admit that I don't iron my sheets or my pillowcases! I do love to hang them on my backyard clothesline and bring them inside in the late afternoon and make up the beds with crisp, fresh, clean sheets.

Mrs. Martha Greene

Ironing Notes

_____
_____
_____
_____
_____
_____
_____

Wrinkles, wrinkles
go away!
Come again
another day!
Who likes to iron?
I cannot say!

Must You Stop Ironing
When Lights Are Needed?

The G-E Twin Convenience Outlet affords double service from a single outlet.

You are ironing. It grows dark. What happens? Must you stop ironing because you cannot have light and run your iron at the same time? Or do you have to move the ironing board to another room?

You can use any number of electrical appliances at the same time if you have real electrical convenience in your home.

The time to insist upon this kind of wiring is —— NOW. Whether you are buying, building, or renting, insist upon sufficient convenience outlets for the many appliances now available to lighten housework and add to comfort —— vacuum cleaners, washing machines, toasters, portable lamps, etc.

Plenty of conveniently located switches are another essential to real electrical convenience —— so that you never need grope through the dark to turn on a light.

Even in the oldest house, complete electrical convenience can be installed at surprisingly little cost with little muss or confusion.

A New Booklet for Home Lovers

How to secure this electrical convenience in each room of your house is told in detail in a booklet prepared for you. This booklet will be sent to you free, together with the name of a nearby electrical contractor qualified to assist you in planning adequate electrical convenience for your home.

What Is Your Address?

The Home of a Hundred Comforts

General Electric Company

General Office
Schenectady, N.Y.

Sales Offices in
all large cities

41-183

27

Laundry & Ironing Table

Make your table to be finished out as wide as a shirt and as long as a pair of pants + enough space to stand your iron up.

To make your table you will need:

hammer, nails, saw, lumber,

4 sturdy pieces of wood for the legs

1 piece for the middle brace

2 long planks for the top

The table should stand about 4-5 inches higher than an ordinary dining table when finished.

Your handy husband can build this for you or this would make a good woodworking project for an older son. It will give him confidence in his abilities to be a good provider and the man of his own home one day.

The legs should be braced according to the sketch below about 12-16 inches from the floor.

This table is very convenient to ironing and once you use it you will not want to replace it with a conventional ironing board. It will take up space and you will need to have a large laundry or spare room to be able to accommodate it. When not used for ironing it could be used as a convenient place to fold laundry. Pad it nicely with some old blankets and a muslin cover and you will be a happy housekeeper!

Laundry & Ironing
Table

If the space cannot be spared for the ironing table to be set up, then try this convenient arrangement:

Cut a thick old blanket to fit your kitchen table. Make a thick cotton ticking cover by cutting it to the size of the table with a bit of extra around the edges of the table. Hem the edges and then sew a 12-inch length of elastic on each of the four corners. Now you have a nice padded cover for your table. It makes a wonderful large and roomy ironing surface. When your ironing is finished, just remove your pad, fold up and store away on a shelf beside your iron. No bulky ironing board to store when not in use!

Ironing Tips

˜ If care is taken with clothing to be thoroughly shaken and hung out neatly on the line, little pressing will be needed for play clothes and linens, if any at all.

˜ Clothes that are dried in the modern convenience of a clothes dryer should be promptly removed to prevent crumbling and wrinkles from setting in.

˜ A good, reliable iron, with the feature of steam, is a necessity for a household. If steam is not a feature on your iron, then a sprinkling of water on the garment will aid in pressing out stubborn wrinkles.

˜ Take care to set the iron on the proper setting for your garments. Use hotter settings for heavy cottons and lighter heat for synthetics and fine fabrics.

˜ To clean build-up on the bottom of the iron, try a damp cloth and a bit of toothpaste. Scour lightly and then wipe clean. To clean a steam iron that has developed deposits, fill tank with white vinegar. Let steam for 5 minutes on high heat, then empty vinegar and rinse once with water. Iron over an old cotton cloth until iron is dry. Fill with clean water the next time you need use of the steam iron.

˜ If you use too hot of an iron on a white cotton garment and get a scorch mark, your remedy is to dip a cotton ball or clean sponge in peroxide and dab the scorched spot. The scorch will quickly disappear and then you can sponge the area with a clean, damp, cotton cloth and iron on as before.

˜ If you like a pleasant scent to your neatly ironed clothes, add a drop of fragrant or essential oil (e.g., lavender) or a bit of your favorite cologne to the water into the steam tank of your iron. The fragrance will steam out of the iron and permeate the garment you are ironing and freshen the air in the closets where the garments are hung. It does not seem to harm the iron.

Household Iron

Purchase date:_____

Brand:_____

Cost:_____

Purchased at:_____

Use this blank page for journaling or attach snippets and clippings for keepsakes.

Hospitality

Use this blank page for journaling or attach snippets and clippings for keepsakes.

" *The beauty of a home is cleanliness.*
The blessing of a home is contentment.
The glory of a home is hospitality."

Use this blank page for journaling or attach snippets and clippings for keepsakes.

On the Duty of Hospitality ~

It is frequently the case, that the social enjoyments of life, with many are never placed in the list of ones duties. Many men allow their professional employments and many mothers the cares of their families, to occupy their whole time, and never imagine when they confess their neglect of social hospitality that they are confessing omissions of sacred duties.
~ Adapted from Catharine E. Beecher's <u>Treatise on Home Economy</u>, 1841

An open home flows from an open heart. There is a big emphasis in the New Testament on hospitality. To be put on the church's list, widows were assessed by five criteria, and one of them was lodging strangers. (1 Timothy 5:9-10). Please note that all 5 criteria were to be practiced in the home. One of the qualifications for elders and deacons is that they be "given to hospitality" (1 Timothy 3:2). We are omitting a sacred duty if we are not practicing hospitality.

Hospitality puts people before things. Don't let your mentality be, "Oh, we'll invite them over as soon as we get the new ____(sofa, dining room table, room remodeled,...) but rather, "Our house is not _____ (finished, fancy, or large...) but come and share what God has given us." Hospitality is serving; saying "my life is yours."

Two things live forever—God's Word and people. Therefore, they should be our top priority for life. It is wrong reasoning to say, "Oh, I care about people and invest in them, so I have no time to keep my home clean and running smoothly." One of the biggest hindrances to hospitality is not keeping an orderly home. If the house is not picked up, you will not invite people over on the spur of the moment. You need to manage your house so you can invest in people. Cleaning is a means to an end, but it also gives great joy and satisfaction in the process!

Discipline yourself to keep an orderly home ~ not a spotless one, mind you, but an ordered one! Determine to make your home a place where anyone can stop by and be welcomed inside. Tidy the house every night before you retire and orderliness will greet you in the morning.

~ *Mrs. Lydia Greene*

Preparing Hearth & Home

To be hospitable is to provide your guests
with a pleasant and sustaining environment.

Ideas for Overnight Guests

◊ Buy toothbrushes when they are buy one, get one free. Tie a ribbon around one and place it on your guest's towel set.

◊ Have a radio/alarm clock in the guest bedroom.

◊ Place a portable fan in the guest room. The gentle, constant noise drowns out the unfamiliar sounds so your guests may sleep easier.

◊ Ask your guests what they like to drink for breakfast before they retire. You can have their favorite drink ready to pour when they come to the table in the morning.

◊ Put brochures of sight-seeing attractions from your area in the guest room so guests can browse through them and decide what they might like to see.

◊ Keep extra rolls of toilet tissue in a basket in the restroom.

Kindness to God's Servants

Before you have missionaries over, fix their children a grab bag to give them as they leave. It will brighten their little lives and give mom and dad a few minutes of quiet as they resume their journey. Ideas for bags: Activity and sticker books, fruit rollups, crayons and coloring books. All can be bought when they are on special discounts.

Help! They are Coming Over to Eat?

Always keep ingredients on hand for a quick and easy meal. You can keep cooked, boneless chicken breast (stir-fried in olive oil and seasoned with taco seasonings), tortillas, and grated cheese in the freezer ready to pull out at a moment's notice. You can quickly fix up some chicken quesadillas for a lunch, supper or Sunday evening snack. Serve with sour cream and salsa. Voila! You have a nice light meal with little fuss.

In the summer, you can stock orange sherbet in the freezer and lemon-lime soda in the pantry for floats. Just add a scoop or two of sherbet to each glass and fill with lemon-lime soda. Purchase some decorative tall glasses and keep some brightly-colored straws on hand. When you serve your Orange-Lime Floats, they will look like an extraordinary drink!

In the winter, I stock up on brownie mixes, because all my children know how to fix them, and by the time we have finished Creamy Tomato Soup and Grilled Cheese Sandwiches (a winter standby at our house), a wonderful chocolate aroma fills the house and we serve warm brownies and ice cream. ◆ *Mrs. Lydia Greene*

The Fare

Sample menus and recipes for serving your guests.

The Prepared Hostess

P	Prepare and Plan ahead.
R	Rejoice in every good thing.
E	Expect your children to have manners.
P	Please your own husband.
A	Artistry ~ Each meal is a work of art.
R	Refresh others.
E	Edify with words round your table.
D	Devotions around the family table.

~ *Mrs. Kimberly Eddy*

Brunch

Egg & Sausage Bake
Fruit Bowl
Blueberry Oat Cake
Nana Muffins
Hot Mocha

Light Lunch

Chicken Salad or Tuna Salad
Potato Pan Rolls
Raw Vegetable Platter
Chips
Lemonade with Tea Cubes

Country Dinner

Parmesan Chicken
Cold Macaroni Salad or Seven-Layer Salad
Corn-on-the-Cob
Jeweled Biscuits
Iced Tea
Strawberry Cake

Holiday Dinner

Baked Ham
Red Rice
Buttered Broccoli Spears
Sweet Potato Souffle
Ambrosia Salad
Posie Rolls
Iced Mint Tea
Mini-Cheesecakes
Almond Nougats
Coffee

Desserts Only

Gail's Carrot Cake
Coconut Chocolate Ring Cake
Candied Apple Pie
Peaches 'n' Cream Pie
Brownie Bars
Butter Nut Bars
Oatmeal Crème Sandwich Cookies
Frosted Mocha Cookies

❧❧ Brunch Recipes ❧❧

Egg & Sausage Bake
Place in buttered 9x13 baking dish:
4 cups cubed bread
2 cups sharp Cheddar cheese, grated
Combine and pour over bread cubes and cheese:
10 eggs, slightly beaten
4 cups milk
1 teaspoon dry mustard
1 teaspoon salt
¼ teaspoon onion powder
sprinkling of black pepper
Sprinkle over egg mixture:
1 pound sausage, browned and drained of excess grease
½ cup fresh tomatoes, peeled and chopped (optional)
Cover and refrigerate overnight. Bake uncovered for 1 hour at 325°.
Make a foil tent if the casserole browns too quickly while baking.
Serves 8-10

Creamy Fruit Bowl
Mix together in a large bowl:
2 cans peach slices, drained of juice
2 apples, peeled and diced
1 can pear pieces, drained of juice
2 cans pineapple tidbits, drained of juice
2 cups green seedless grapes, washed and stemmed
1 cup red seedless grapes, washed and stemmed
1 small bag mini-marshmallows
Mix in a separate small bowl and fold into fruit mixture:
2 tablespoons mayonnaise
1 ~ 12 ounce tub of whipped topping
Serves 12-15

Blueberry Oat Cake

Beat until smooth in a large bowl:
2 eggs
2 cups buttermilk
1 cup brown sugar, packed
½ cup vegetable oil
Combine and add to the egg mixture above:
2 cups unbleached all-purpose flour
2 teaspoons baking powder
1 teaspoon baking soda
1 teaspoon ground cinnamon
½ teaspoon salt
Beat with beaters on a low speed for 2 minutes.
Gently fold in:
2 cups quick-cooking oatmeal flakes
2 cups fresh or frozen blueberries
1 cup walnuts, chopped (optional)
Put batter into a greased and floured bundt or tube cake pan. Bake for 45-50 minutes at 375° or until pick inserted in center comes out clean. Cool for 10 minutes and then remove carefully from pan onto a wire rack to cool completely. Dust with confectioner's sugar with a sifter.
Serves 12-16

Hot Mocha

Place in a large saucepan and bring to a simmering boil:
¼ cup baking cocoa (unsweetened)
½ cup sugar
½ cup water
pinch of salt
3 teaspoons instant coffee granules
Simmer while stirring for 2-3 minutes. Then add in:
4 cups milk
¼ teaspoon vanilla flavoring
Do not boil! Remove from heat as soon as milk has heated through.
Serve piping hot.
Serves 5. Multiply recipe to serve more.

Nana Muffins

In small bowl, combine and set aside topping mixture:
¼ cup brown sugar
3 tablespoons all-purpose flour
2 tablespoons soft butter
4 tablespoons nuts, finely chopped (optional)

In mixing bowl, combine:
2 cups unbleached all-purpose flour
1 cup sugar
1 teaspoon baking powder
½ teaspoon salt
½ teaspoon baking soda
¼ teaspoon ground cinnamon
In a separate mixing bowl, blend together:
2 eggs
¼ cup butter, melted
2 very ripe bananas, mashed
Add in dry ingredients and stir until ingredients are incorporated. Do
not over mix. Fill paper-lined muffin pans with batter, filling cups only
¾ full.   Sprinkle each muffin with topping. Bake for 25 minutes at 375°.
Makes 12 regular-size muffins, 24 mini-muffins, 6 jumbo muffins.

Brunch (brunch) *n.* [BR(EAKFAST) + (L)UNCH]
[Colloq.] a late first meal of the day that takes the place
of both breakfast and lunch.

Webster's New World Dictionary of the American Language

❧ Simple Lunch Recipes ❧

Chicken Salad

1 ¾ cup chicken, cooked and finely chopped
1 cup chopped walnuts
¾ cup mayonnaise
1 stalk of celery, finely chopped
1 small onion, finely chopped
1 teaspoon salt
½ teaspoon garlic powder

Combine all ingredients and refrigerate until serving. Split rolls and spoon inside or use as a cracker spread. A food processor with a blade is useful in finely chopping ingredients.
Serves 4. Multiply recipe to serve more guests.

Tuna Salad

3 ~ 12 ounce cans tuna, drained
1 ½ cups mayonnaise
1 ½ cups chopped cashews
1 tablespoon onion, chopped
3 tablespoons sweet red pepper, chopped
3 tablespoons sweet green pepper, chopped
3 tablespoons sour cream
1 tablespoon vinegar
¾ teaspoon salt

Combine all ingredients. Makes a nice sandwich filler for rolls or topping for crackers. This can be served on a lettuce leaf lined with chow mein noodles if you care to serve it without rolls.
Serves 10-12. Reduce recipe for serving fewer guests.

Potato Pan Rolls

Bring to boil in a small saucepan and simmer
20 minutes or until tender:
2 medium potatoes, peeled and quartered
1 ½ cups water
Drain, reserving 1 cup of potato water. Mash potatoes and measure out
1 cup mashed potatoes for recipe. Cool potato water to 115°.
In a mixing bowl, add in:
2 heaping tablespoons yeast
1 teaspoon sugar
1 cup potato water (115°)
Let stand for 5 minutes, stirring lightly to dissolve yeast.
Add in:
1 cup mashed potatoes, slightly cooled
½ cup butter, melted
½ cup honey
¼ cup vegetable oil
2 eggs
2 teaspoons salt
1 ½ cups unbleached all-purpose flour
Beat until smooth. Stir in enough remaining flour (about 5-6 cups) to
make a soft dough. Knead 6-8 minutes until smooth and elastic.
Turn onto floured surface. Divide dough into 30 pieces, shaping each
into a ball. Place 10 balls each into 3 greased, 9-inch round pans. Cover
with oiled plastic wrap and let rise until doubled in size, about 45
minutes. Bake for 20-25 minutes at 400° or until lightly browned.
Remove to wire racks to cool.
Makes 30 rolls. Serves 15.

Lunch (lunch) *n.* 1. any light meal; esp. the regular
midday meal between breakfast and dinner

Webster's New World Dictionary of the American Language

Raw Vegetable Platter

Arrange on an attractive platter:
Carrots, peeled and cut into sticks
Cucumbers, peeled and cut into spears
Broccoli florets, (wash and trim florets off heads of broccoli)
Celery ribs, cut into 4-inch lengths
Green olives on toothpicks
Kosher dill pickle spears
Bread 'n' butter pickle chunks

Lemonade with Tea Cubes

Heat together in a small saucepan, stirring until sugar dissolves:
1 cup sugar
4 cups water
Cool and then stir in:
Juice of 8 lemons
Pour into a pitcher. Refrigerate.
Place in small saucepan and bring to boil:
3 cups water
15 whole cloves
4 (2-inch) cinnamon sticks
Remove from heat and pour over 8 regular-size tea bags. Let stand for
10 minutes. Discard spices and tea bags and add in:
3 cups cold water. Pour into ice cube trays and freeze.
Makes approximately 4 trays of tea cubes.
To serve:
Fill tall glasses with tea cubes. Pour lemonade over cubes
and garnish each glass with lemon slices.
Multiply recipe as needed to make larger quantities.

❧❧ Country Dinner ❧❧

Parmesan Chicken

Mix in a bowl:
2 cups of instant potato flakes
2 tablespoons parsley flakes
4 tablespoons Parmesan cheese
pinch of salt and black pepper
Melt 1 stick butter in a small saucepan.
Dip 16 skinless chicken pieces in melted butter. Melt more butter if
needed. Sprinkle butter-coated chicken pieces with salt.
Then coat each chicken piece in potato flake mixture. Place chicken
pieces on foil-lined baking sheets in one layer. Bake for 1 hour and 15
minutes at 400° or until crispy and lightly browned. Turn chicken
pieces once after 40 minutes so both sides brown evenly.
Serves 12-14.

Cold Macaroni Salad

Cook in boiling water for 8 minutes and then drain:
2 cups elbow macaroni
Rinse in cold water. Combine in a small bowl:
½ cup mayonnaise
¼ cup milk
1 teaspoon sugar
1 tablespoon yellow prepared mustard
2 tablespoons white vinegar
Add in:
2 cups cucumber, peeled and cubed
1 cup cherry tomatoes, halved
3 hard-boiled eggs, sliced
2 stalks celery, finely chopped
3 cups cheddar cheese, cubed
1 cup green olives, sliced
Combine gently and add in cooked and cooled macaroni.
Add salt and pepper to taste.
Refrigerate until serving.
Serves 10-12

45

Seven-Layer Salad

Layer in a large, oblong glass dish in the order listed:
½ head iceberg or romaine lettuce, coarsely chopped
2 stalks celery, diced
1 cup sweet green bell pepper, diced
1 medium red sweet onion, thinly sliced
2 cups English peas
(Run warm water over frozen English peas to thaw
slightly or use fresh raw garden peas).
Mix together in a small bowl:
1 ½ cups mayonnaise
2 teaspoons sugar
Spread over layers carefully.
Cover over dressing layer with grated Cheddar cheese.
Top salad with crumbled, crisply-cooked bacon.
Garnish all sides with small cherry tomatoes.
Cover and refrigerate until serving.
Serves 10-12.

Corn-on-the-Cob

Have a large pot of water boiling on the stove. Drop in corn cobs that
have been shucked and washed free of silks. You may also put frozen ears
of corn in the boiling water. There is no need to thaw them. Let simmer
for 7-10 minutes and serve hot with butter and salt.
Allow 1 large ear per person.

Iced Tea

Bring to a boil in a saucepan:
3 cups water
3 family-size tea bags
Remove from heat and let stand 10 minutes.
Remove tea bags and add in 1-2 cups
sugar (depends on sweetness desired). Stir to dissolve.
Pour into a gallon-size pitcher and fill to the top with cold water.
Refrigerate until serving time. Makes 1 gallon.

Jeweled Biscuits

Place in a small bowl, stir and set aside:
1 heaping tablespoon yeast
5 tablespoons warm water (110°)
Place in a large mixing bowl:
5 cups unbleached all-purpose flour
¼ cup sugar
4 teaspoons baking powder
1 teaspoon salt
Mix until blended and then cut in until you have coarse crumbs:
1 cup vegetable shortening
Add in to crumbly flour mixture:
1 ½ cups warm buttermilk (110°)
yeast mixture that was set aside
Stir to combine and turn out onto a floured surface.
Knead by hand, lightly, about 6 times.
Pat out to a ½-inch thickness. Cut out with a biscuit cutter
and transfer to a large, greased baking sheet. Slit the center of
each biscuit with kitchen scissors making a 1-inch cut halfway
through the center. Use your thumb to make an indention at
the slit opening and fill with a scant teaspoon of fruit jam or
preserves. Blackberry and strawberry are both delicious!
Let biscuits stand on baking sheets for 15 minutes and then
bake for 20 minutes at 400° or until golden brown on tops.
Makes 30 biscuits. Reduce recipe for a smaller batch.

Dinner (din'er) *n.* [ME.diner<OFr. Disner, inf.
Used as *n.*] 1. The chief meal of the day, whether
eaten in the evening or about noon.

Webster's New World Dictionary of the American Language

Strawberry Cake

Beat all ingredients together in a mixing bowl:
2 ½ cups self-rising flour
1 ½ cups vegetable oil
4 eggs
2 cups sugar
1 cup buttermilk
1 teaspoon vinegar
1 teaspoon vanilla
Pour into a greased and floured 9"x 13" pan.
Bake for 40-45 minutes at 350°.
Remove cake from oven. Punch holes in cake when out of the oven with
a wooden spoon handle. Drizzle juice from drained strawberries*(used
in frosting) over cake. Frost when completely cooled.
Store in refrigerator.

~ Frosting Recipe ~

1 teaspoon vanilla extract
1 cup sugar
8 ounces sour cream
8 ounces whipped topping
2 ~ 10 ounce packages frozen *strawberries, thawed and drained
Blend all ingredients until fluffy and smooth.
Serves 12

✌ Folding Elegant Napkins ✌
Make a Fan:

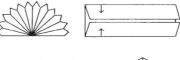

Fold top and bottom edges to the center.
Fold top and bottom edges to the middle once more.
Pleat firmly from the left edge.
Press to make a sharp crease with a hot, steam iron, spraying
with starch while pressing. Starch helps the fan hold shape.
Slide a pretty napkin ring or tie a ribbon near the base
and fan out the pleats to make a fan design.

❦❧ Holiday Dinner Recipes ❦❧

Baked Ham

Place ham fat side up in a baking crock. Add in 2 cups of water. Bake covered in a slow oven (325°) for approximately 3 hours or until very tender. Reserve drippings. Carve and place on platter. Refrigerate any leftover portions. 8 pound ham will serve 14.

Red Rice

Place in a saucepan, cover, and bring to a simmer:
1 cup white rice, uncooked
1 ¼ cups liquid drippings from baked ham
1 cup water
1 tablespoon butter
pinch of pepper
Simmer for 20 minutes on medium-low.
Salt only after cooking, if needed.
Serves 4. Multiply recipe to serve more guests.

Buttered Broccoli Spears

Wash heads of broccoli. Cut and trim off large, tough stalks. Drop florets with tender stalk attached into a large saucepan of boiling water. Cover and simmer for 15 minutes or until stalks are fork-tender. Drain off water. Top with pats of butter. Sprinkle with salt. If desired, sprinkle with slivered almonds.
1 head of broccoli serves 4.

*" Table settings and embellishments give off a "mood " to the diner
of peace or festivity, depending on the colors, textures and styles.
The hostess can also dress to coordinate with the color and style
of her table in keeping with the event she is celebrating."*
❧   Mrs. Lydia Sherman
~ Used with permission ~
~ Lady Lydia of Ladies Against Feminism ~

Sweet Potato Soufflè

Mix together in a large mixing bowl with an electric beater until smooth:

3 cups cooked and mashed sweet potatoes

¾ cup sugar

½ teaspoon salt

2 eggs, well beaten

¼ cup butter, melted

½ cup milk

1 teaspoon vanilla extract

Pour into a greased, glass casserole dish (oven-proof).

Use 1 large dish or 2 small dishes.

Mix in a small bowl:

1 cup brown sugar

¼ cup flour

1 cup chopped pecans or walnuts

3 tablespoons soft butter

Sprinkle over potato mixture.

Freeze for later use or bake immediately for 40 minutes at 350°.

If frozen, thaw in refrigerator overnight and bake

the next day before serving time.

Ambrosia Salad

Mix together in a large mixing bowl:

1 cup sour cream

1 cup whipped topping

3 cups pineapple tidbits, drained

3 cups mandarin oranges, drained

½ cup flaked coconut

Chill before serving.

Serves 4-6.

Multiply recipe to serve large groups.

Posie Rolls

Place in small saucepan and heat to 120°:
2 cups sour cream
1 ½ cups water
1 cup butter
Place in a large kitchen mixer equipped with a dough hook:
6 cups unbleached bread flour
3 tablespoons sugar
3 teaspoons salt
4 tablespoons yeast
Add in:
4 eggs, well beaten
warm sour cream mixture (115°-120°)
Begin mixing on medium speed and add in:
2 cups whole wheat flour
more bread flour to make a soft dough
Knead for 6 minutes. Let rise until puffy and then punch down.
Place dough onto a large, oiled baking sheet and flatten out to 1 ¼
inch thick. Cut out rolls with a small drinking cup (diameter about
3 inches) with rim floured for easier cutting. Place cut rolls onto a
greased baking sheet, touching each other. Let rise until puffy, about 45
minutes. Brush carefully with 1 beaten egg mixed with
2 tablespoons water. Sprinkle tops of rolls with
sesame or poppy seeds.   Bake for 13-15 minutes at 400°.
Yield depends on what size rolls are cut. Makes a large batch.

Iced Mint Tea

Bring to a boil in a saucepan:
3 cups water
3 family-size tea bags
Remove from heat and let stand 10 minutes.
Remove tea bags, add in 1-2 cups sugar (depends on sweetness desired).
Stir to dissolve.
In separate saucepan boil for 5 minutes:
1 cup fresh peppermint leaves, washed
2 cups water
Let stand 15 minutes. Discard peppermint leaves and add into tea mixture. Pour tea and mint brew into a 1 gallon size pitcher and fill to the
top with cold water. Refrigerate until serving time.
Makes 1 gallon.

51

Mini-Cheesecakes

Line muffin tins with foil paper cup liners.
In a large mixing bowl, beat with electric beaters
until fluffy and smooth:
8 ounces cream cheese, softened
1 teaspoon vanilla extract
1/3 cup juice from fresh-squeezed lemons
1 ~ 14 ounce can sweetened condensed milk
Place a vanilla wafer in the bottom of each muffin liner.
Spoon and mound the filling on top of each wafer.
Chill. Garnish with blueberries, cherries,
or chocolate shavings if desired.

Almond Nougats

Place in mixing bowl:
1 cup butter, softened
½ cup confectioner's powdered sugar
1 teaspoon vanilla extract
2 cups unbleached, all-purpose flour
pinch of salt
¾ cup sliced almonds, crushed

Mix all together with clean hands until all ingredients are incorporated.
Form balls about 1 inch in diameter. Flatten just slightly. Place on
parchment-lined baking sheets. Bake for 12 minutes at 400°. Do not
brown. Let cool for 10 minutes and then gently dip and roll in powdered
sugar. Makes 36 nougats.

Coffee For A Crowd

Grind 1 pound of fresh coffee beans in a coffee grinder. Place in a
cheesecloth bag that will give room for grounds to swell. Double the size
of the grounds should be sufficient. Before serving, have ready a large
pot, holding 6 quarts of cold water. Bring the water to a boil close to
serving time. Place the coffee-filled cheesecloth bag into the boiling water. Let it stand 10 minutes. Agitate the bag a few times during the 10
minutes. Remove bag. Pour hot coffee from brewing pot into a lovely
china teapot to serve your guests. Serve at once with cream and sugar
cubes. Serves 35-40 guests. Reduce recipe to serve fewer guests.

❧❧ Desserts Only ❧❧

Gail's Carrot Cake

Grease and flour two 9-inch cake pans <u>or</u> one 9"x 13" baking pan.
Place in large mixing bowl and beat with electric mixer for 1 minute:

4 eggs

1 ½ cups cooking oil

2 cups sugar

Mix together in a smaller mixing bowl:

2 cups unbleached all-purpose flour

1 teaspoon baking powder

1 teaspoon baking soda

2 teaspoons cinnamon

¼ teaspoon salt

Add flour mixture to egg mixture and beat for 2 minutes. Add in:

3 cups grated carrots

2 cups chopped walnuts (optional)

Put batter into prepared pans and bake for 30-40 minutes at 375° or until
pick inserted in center comes out clean. Let cool 15 minutes. Carefully
remove from pan onto serving plate. Frost with icing. If using 2 layers
place some frosting between layers and all over top. Garnish top of cake
with finely crushed walnuts.

~ Icing ~

Mix together in a medium mixing bowl until smooth and creamy:

½ cup soft butter (1 stick)

1 ~ 8 ounce cream cheese, softened

5 cups powdered confectioner's sugar

2 teaspoons vanilla extract

1 teaspoon juice from fresh-squeezed lemon

One 9"x 13" cake will serve 12-15.

Coconut Chocolate Ring Cake

Grease and flour a 10-inch bundt cake pan.
In a small mixing bowl, beat together until smooth:
¼ cup sugar
1 teaspoon vanilla extract
1 egg
1 ~ 8 ounce package cream cheese, softened
Stir into the cream cheese mixture and then set mixture aside:
½ cup flaked coconut
1 cup chocolate chips
Place in a large mixer bowl:
2 cups sugar
2 eggs
1 cup cooking oil
Beat with electric beaters for 1 minute on high speed.
Add in:
3 cups flour
¾ cup unsweetened baking cocoa powder
2 teaspoons baking soda
2 teaspoons baking powder
1 ½ teaspoons salt
1 cup hot coffee (use 1 cup hot water + 1 teaspoon instant coffee granules)
1 cup buttermilk
1 teaspoon vanilla
Beat with electric beater for 3 more minutes on medium speed.
Stir in by hand:
1 cup chopped walnuts or pecans
Pour half the batter into the prepared pan; carefully spoon cream cheese/
coconut mixture over the batter. Top with remaining batter. Bake for
70 75 minutes at 350° or until top of cake springs back when pressed
lightly with your finger. Cool for 15 minutes; then carefully remove from
pan onto a serving plate. Cool completely and drizzle with glazing.

~ Glazing ~
Mix in a small mixing bowl until smooth:
1 cup powdered confectioner's sugar
3 tablespoons unsweetened baking cocoa powder
2 tablespoons butter, softened
2 teaspoons vanilla extract
2 tablespoons hot water
Makes 1 large bundt cake. Serves 14-16.

Candied Apple Pie

For this recipe you will need a pastry for a double crust pie.
Place in a large bowl:
6 cups thinly sliced, peeled apples
2 tablespoons lime juice
Combine together in a small bowl and then add to the
apples, tossing lightly:
¾ cup sugar
¼ cup unbleached all-purpose flour
½ teaspoon ground cinnamon
¼ teaspoon salt
Place bottom pastry in a 9-inch pie plate; fill with apple mixture. Dot with a few pats of butter and then cover with top pastry. Flute the edges with a high rim and cut steam vents. Bake for 45 minutes at 400° or until crust is golden brown and apples are tender.
While pie is baking, prepare candy topping.
Combine in a small saucepan, stir, and bring to a boil:
¼ cup butter
½ cup packed brown sugar
2 teaspoons of heavy cream or evaporated milk
½ cup pecans, chopped
Remove from heat source and pour over top crust when pie is removed from oven. Return to the oven and bake 4-7 more minutes or until topping is bubbly. Serve pie warm with a small scoop of vanilla ice cream. Serves 6-8

Peaches 'n' Cream Pie

Combine in a saucepan:
¾ cup sugar
3 tablespoons cornstarch
Add in and cook over medium heat until thickened:
1 cup boiling water
Remove from heat when thickened and add in:
1 ~ 3 ounce packet peach-flavored Jello™
Mix well and cool until lukewarm.
Place in a baked, cooled pie pastry shell:
3 cups fresh sliced peaches
Pour cooled, thickened mixture over the peaches in shell.
Chill until firm in refrigerator.
Serve wedges of pie with large dollops of whipped cream.

Brownie Bars

Place into a large mixing bowl and stir to combine:

2 cups sugar

4 eggs, beaten

¾ cup cooking oil

½ cup unsweetened baking cocoa powder

1 ¾ cups unbleached all-purpose flour

1 teaspoon salt

1 teaspoon vanilla extract

Place batter into a well-greased 9"x 13" baking pan. Sprinkle top of batter with 1 ½ cups chocolate chips. Bake for 20-25 minutes at 350°. Let cool and cut into bars. Makes 15-18 bars.

Butter Nut Bars

Place into a mixing bowl and stir to combine:

1 cup margarine or butter

¼ cup crunchy style peanut butter

1 cup sugar

1 egg

1 tablespoon vanilla extract

2 cups all-purpose, unbleached flour

Add in:

1 cup chocolate chips

1 cup peanut butter chips

Spread batter into a greased 9"x 13" baking pan. Bake for 20-25 minutes at 350°. Do not overbake. Cool and cut in bars.

Makes 15-18 bars depending on size cut.

∾ Handmade Paper Doilies ॐ

Take a circle of paper the size you would like your doily.

Fold in half once, then again, then one more time.

Cut outer edge with decorative pattern-edged scissors and paper punches to create lacy designs. Unfold and press with a hot, dry iron.

Use to line your serving plate of freshly-baked cookies or brownies.

~ Resource ~

Scrapbook specialty stores carry a variety of patterned-edge scissors and paper-punches in decorative designs.

Frosted Mocha Cookies

Melt together in a small saucepan:
½ cup vegetable shortening
2 ~ 1-ounce squares unsweetened chocolate
Cool for 10 minutes and put into a mixing bowl and then add in and mix:
1 cup brown sugar
1 egg
1 teaspoon vanilla extract
½ cup buttermilk
Mix together in a smaller mixing bowl, removing any lumps:
1 ½ cups unbleached, all-purpose flour
½ teaspoon baking powder
½ teaspoon baking soda
¼ teaspoon salt
Add into chocolate mixture and stir to combine. Stir in:
½ cup chopped walnuts
1 cup chocolate chips
Drop by teaspoonfuls onto a greased cookie sheet. Bake for 10 minutes
at 375°. Remove with a spatula to a wire rack to cool.
When cooled, frost with mocha frosting and garnish with a walnut half.

~ Mocha Frosting ~

Beat in a small bowl until smooth and spreadable:
¼ cup butter
2 tablespoons unsweetened baking cocoa powder
2 teaspoons instant coffee powder
pinch salt
2 ½ cups powdered confectioner's sugar
1 ½ teaspoons vanilla
2 tablespoons milk
Add a bit more milk to make spreadable if needed.

Oatmeal Crème Sandwich Cookies

Cream together in a mixing bowl:
½ cup margarine
½ cup vegetable shortening
¼ cup peanut butter
½ cup sugar
½ cup brown sugar
2 eggs
1 teaspoon vanilla extract
Add in and stir to combine:
1 cup unbleached, all-purpose flour
½ cup whole wheat flour
1 teaspoon baking soda
½ teaspoon salt
2 cups rolled oats

Using a serving spoon, drop onto a greased cookie sheet and flatten slightly. Place only 6 cookies per large cookie sheet, leaving room for cookies to bake and spread without touching. Bake for 10-12 minutes at 375°. Remove to wire racks to cool. When cooled, put 2 cookies together in a sandwich fashion with crème filling spread in the middle.

~ Crème Filling ~

Beat together until smooth and creamy:
1 ~ 8 ounce package cream cheese, softened
¼ cup butter, softened
¼ cup peanut butter
1 ~ 7 ounce jar of marshmallow cream
2 tablespoons milk
1 cup confectioner's powdered sugar
1 teaspoon maple flavoring

Like Mother Makes

Our Merry Guests

A record of guests that graced our home.

Date ~   Name ~   Occasion ~

——————   ————————————————————————   ——————————
——————   ————————————————————————   ——————————
——————   ————————————————————————   ——————————
——————   ————————————————————————   ——————————
——————   ————————————————————————   ——————————
——————   ————————————————————————   ——————————
——————   ————————————————————————   ——————————
——————   ————————————————————————   ——————————
——————   ————————————————————————   ——————————
——————   ————————————————————————   ——————————
——————   ————————————————————————   ——————————
——————   ————————————————————————   ——————————
——————   ————————————————————————   ——————————
——————   ————————————————————————   ——————————
——————   ————————————————————————   ——————————
——————   ————————————————————————   ——————————
——————   ————————————————————————   ——————————
——————   ————————————————————————   ——————————
——————   ————————————————————————   ——————————
——————   ————————————————————————   ——————————
——————   ————————————————————————   ——————————

Date ~   Name ~   Occasion ~

Date ~   Name ~   Occasion ~
_____   _____   _____
_____   _____   _____
_____   _____   _____
_____   _____   _____
_____   _____   _____
_____   _____   _____
_____   _____   _____
_____   _____   _____
_____   _____   _____
_____   _____   _____
_____   _____   _____
_____   _____   _____
_____   _____   _____
_____   _____   _____
_____   _____   _____
_____   _____   _____
_____   _____   _____
_____   _____   _____
_____   _____   _____
_____   _____   _____
_____   _____   _____
_____   _____   _____
_____   _____   _____
_____   _____   _____
_____   _____   _____
_____   _____   _____

61

Use this blank page for journaling or attach snippets and clippings for keepsakes.

Home Duties

Use this blank page for journaling or attach snippets and clippings for keepsakes.

" *The more difficult the duty. . . . .the*
more need of singing! "

Use this blank page for journaling or attach snippets and clippings for keepsakes.

The morning, afternoon, and evening duties beckon us. We have days where
we are disheartened, days when our strength seems to fail us, when we are
so tired of our duties, our tasks at hand seem daunting and endless.
These precious reflections from yesteryear make us
stop....reminisce....and remember to keep the right perspective.

 # Reflections

Children will not trouble you long. They grow up—nothing on earth grows up so fast as children. It was but yesterday and that lad was playing with tops, a buoyant boy. He is a man and gone now. There is no more childhood for him or for us. Life has claimed him. When a beginning is made, it is like a raveling stocking; stitch by stitch gives way till all are gone. The house has not a child in it—there is no more noise in the hall—or boys to rush in pell mell; it is very orderly now. There are no more skates or sleds, bats, balls, or strings left scattered about. Things are neat enough now. There is no delay for sleepy folks. There is no longer any task, before you lie down, of looking after anybody and tucking up the bedclothes. There are no diapers to settle, nobody to get off to school, no complaint, no opportunities for impossible things, no rip to mend, no fingers to tie up, no faces to be washed or collars to be arranged. There was never such peace in the house! It would sound like music to have some feet to clatter down the front stairs. Oh, for some children's noise! What used to ail us that we were hushing their loud laugh, checking their noisy frolic and reproving their slamming and banging of doors? We wish our neighbors would only lend us an urchin or two to make a little noise in the premises. A home without children is like a lantern and no candle; a garden and no flowers; a vine and no grapes; a brook and no water gurgling and gushing in its channel. We want to be tired, to be vexed, to be run over, to hear children at work with all its varieties.

~published in 1879~

~ from ~
The Royal Path of Life: Aims and Aids to Success and Happiness
By
T.L. Hames, A.M. & L.W. Yaggy, M.S.
Western Publishing House, Philadelphia, PA

Morning Duties for the Homekeeper

And say to mothers what a holy charge is theirs;
With what a kingly power their love might rule the fountains of the newborn mind.
Warn them to wake at early dawn and sow good seed
Before the world has sown its tares.

By~ Mrs. Sigourney ~ 1882

This is a sample listing of duties for the morning. Each home will have a variance of duties to be accomplished according to the lifestyle and accommodations. If diligence is taken to arise early and work with vigor for the first few hours of the day, the day will wear on with ease and the household will run smoothly.

- Rise and smile! What a wonderful day and how blessed you are to have been given one more day of life. Begin it by thanking the Lord God for your family and your life and ask for help to live your day as pleasing to Him.

- Make your bed as soon as you arise.

- Wash and dress for the day.

- Begin a load of laundry.

- Wake the family.

- Prepare breakfast and gather the family to partake.

- Look over the daily meal schedule and begin early preparations that will be necessary to make the day run smoother.

- Tidy the house and do any scheduled house-cleaning chores. If done in the earlier morning hours, the home will stay neater throughout the day. Children of the home are a great help in this area if they have been trained properly.

Afternoon Duties for the Homekeeper

One thing at a time,
And that done well,
Is a very good rule
As many can tell.
~ Unknown ~

The afternoon of a homekeeper can be the most profitable time of the day if it is
not squandered in frivolous activities. Many household duties can be seen to
during this time, but you must take care not to neglect the children.
Give them the attention they require.

☙ Prepare and serve lunch to the family.

☙ Tidy the kitchen and make more preparations to make the evening meal on time for your family.

☙ Use this afternoon time for activities and hobbies you may enjoy. Some suggestions:
> ~ Sewing
> ~ Mending
> ~ Gardening
> ~ Ironing
> ~ Home Decorating

☙ Take a brisk 15 minute walk and enjoy the outdoors. It will improve your strength for the remainder of the day. Don't forget to wear a straw hat in warmer weather.

Contributed by ❧ *Mrs. Sharon Castlebury*

Evening Duties for the Homekeeper

The whippoorwill has sung his song, the family has been fed.
And tho' the day has been so long, we have a soft, warm bed.
As we rest our tired souls, the Lord will vigil keep.
The fireside burns with amber coals, while we slumber deep.

by ~ Martha H. Greene ~

This is a sample of duties for the evenings. Each home will have a variance
in the duties to be accomplished according to lifestyle and accommodations.
If diligence is taken to complete the last few tasks of the day,
the next morning's sun will seem to shine brighter on the new day.

- Serve the evening meal you have prepared for your family.

- Take care to put your kitchen in order. Rising to a new day and its various duties seems so much easier when you arise to a tidy kitchen.

- Set aside foods needed for tomorrow's meals. Hand out the vitamins needed for each family member.

- Take care of personal toiletries and make sure the younger children have washed and taken care of their teeth.

- Relax and rest with the family circle and revel in each other's company. Evenings spent reading as a family make for fond memories. Before retiring for the night, be sure to start your "Moon Tea" for the next day. Simply place 4 family-size tea bags in 1 quart filled with water. Cover tightly with a lid. By noon the next day it will be ready to finish. After removing the tea bags, add 1 cup of sugar and enough water to measure 1 gallon. Refrigerate and enjoy.

Contributed by ~ *Mrs. Sharon Castlebury*

Dutiful Notes

"*Whatever you do -- Do with your might!*
Things done by halves are never done right."

~ Saying from a wise old woman ~

Our Home

Paste
Photograph
Here

Date: _____

72

Duty Ever At Hand

Duty embraces man's whole existence. It begins in the home, where, on the one hand, there is the duty which children owe to their parents and the duty which parents owe their children on the other hand. There surely can be no more important duties to ponder over long and earnestly, than those relating to the home, the duty of patience, of courtesy one to the other, the interest in each other's welfare, the duty of self-control, of learning to bear and forbear.

Children should be trained to behave at home as you would have them behave abroad. It is the home life which they act out when away. If this is rude, gruff, and lacking in civility, they will be lacking in all that constitutes true refinement, and thus most painfully reflect on the home training when in the presence of strangers. In the actions of children, strangers can read a history of the home life. It tells of duty undone, of turmoil and strife, of fretful women and impatient men; or it speaks of a home of love and peace, where patience sits enthroned in the hearts of all its members and each is mindful of his or her duty towards the other.

The domestic fireside is a seminary of infinite importance. It is important because it is universal, and because the education it bestows, woven with the wool of childhood, gives color to the whole texture of life. There are but few who can receive the honors of a college education but all are graduates of the heart. The learning of the university may fade from recollection, its classic lore may be lost from the halls of memory; but the simple lessons of home, enameled upon the heart of childhood, defy the rust of years, and outlive the more mature but less vivid pictures of after days. So deep, so lasting are the impressions of early life that you often see a man in the events of childhood, while all the wide space between that and the present hour is a forgotten waste. It must be remembered that the largest and most important part of the education of children, whether for good or evil, is carried on at home, often unconsciously in their amusements, and under the daily influence of what they see and hear about them. One cannot tell what duties their children may be called to perform in life. They must be taught to cultivate their faculties, and to exercise all their senses to choose the good and refuse the evil.

Adapted from ~ The Golden Gems of Life ~ Gathered Jewels for the Home Circle
by S.C. Ferguson and E. A. Allen
Central Publishing House, Cincinnati ~ 1882 ~

Pondering the Changing Seasons of My Life

_____

_____

_____

_____

_____

_____

_____

_____

_____

_____

_____

_____

_____

_____

_____

_____

_____

_____

_____

_____

_____

_____

Date ~ _____

Children's Duty to Parents

The duties of children to parents are far too little considered. As the children grow up the parents lean on them much earlier than either imagine. In the passage of years the children gain experience and strength. But with the parents! The cares of a long life bow the form, and the strong are again made weak. It is now that the duties of children assume their grandest forms. It is not sufficient to simply give them a home to make their declining years comfortable. While supplying their physical wants, their hearts may be famishing for some expression of love from you. If you think they have outgrown theses desires, you are mistaken. There is always a liability, where sons and daughters have gone from the home of their childhood, and have formed homes of their own, gradually to lose the old attachments and cease to pay those attentions to parents which were so easy and natural in the olden time.

New association, new thoughts, new cares all come in, filling mind and heart and if special pains be not taken they thrust out the old love. This ought never to be! Children should remember that the change is in them and not with those they left behind. They have every thing that is new, such that is attractive in the present and bright and in the future; but the parents' hearts cling to the past and most in memory. When children go away they know not and never will know, until they experience it themselves, what it cost to give them up and what vacancy they left behind. You may disappoint the ambition of your parents, you may be unable to distinguish yourself as you fondly hoped; but let this not swerve you from a determination to be a son or daughter of whose moral character they need never be ashamed. Begin early to cultivate a habit of thoughtfulness and consideration for others, especially for those you are commanded to honor. Can you begrudge a few extra steps for the parents who never stopped to number those hours you demanded during your helpless infancy?

~ Adapted from ~
The Golden Gems of Life
by ~ S. C. Ferguson and E. A. Allen
Central Publishing House, Cincinnati, 1882

Snippets

Snip & paste
items for
memories
around
this page.

 Clippings

Clip & paste
items to
save
around
this page.

Use this blank page for journaling or attach snippets and clippings for keepsakes.

First Aid
in the
Home

Use this blank page for journaling or attach snippets and clippings for keepsakes.

"Could I ease one from her aching?
Tenderly comfort a tiny one's pain?
Then my tending shan't be in vain."

Medicinal Cupboard

Every home needs a cupboard or box with supplies to treat common ailments and minor accidents that will certainly occur.

~ Suggested Supply List ~

◊ thermometer
◊ fever/pain reliever (adult & child)
◊ antacid tablets
◊ antihistimine tablets
◊ antibiotic ointment
◊ bandaids in assorted sizes
◊ gauze & adhesive tape
◊ anti-itch cream
◊ hydrogen peroxide
◊ ace bandage
◊ cough syrup
◊ cotton balls
◊ cotton swabs
◊ tweezers
◊ sun block
◊ aloe-vera gel (keep refrigerated)
◊ sterile eye wash

~ Mini First-Aid Kit for Travel or Vehicle ~

◊ bandaids
◊ antibiotic ointment
◊ pain reliever tablets
◊ antacid tablets
◊ insect sting ointment
◊ cotton balls & swabs
◊ hydrogen peroxide
◊ gauze & tape
◊ small scissors & tweezers

Emergency Care

Situations arise in life that are a crisis and are considered emergencies.
This would be a situation that will not wait!
A life may hang in the balance and you must respond accordingly.

~ Bleeding ~

For minor bleeding apply direct pressure for 1 minute. When stopped, take care not to disturb the site or bleeding may begin again. In the event of major bleeding, apply direct pressure for 10 minutes while telephoning emergency services.

~ Blocked Airway ~

If someone in your care has an obstruction to the air passage, run a finger down the side of the mouth then across, so as not to jam something farther down, when checking for an obstruction. Turn a child over your lap and slap sharply between the shoulder blades two or three times. If there is no obstruction, blowing directly into the face may cause him to inhale. Learn the Heimlich procedure to use with teens and adults. If anyone in your care stops breathing, call emergency services immediately.

~ Head Injury ~

Do not give any pain medication until the situation has been evaluated by professional medical personnel. A severe blow to the head needs immediate professional attention. A minor injury to the head requires alertness of the caregiver. Keep head of the injured elevated. Check to see that pupils react to light similarly. Improper pupil response and or nausea indicates a concussion and will need immediate medical attention.

~ Broken Bones ~

An obviously broken bone needs immediate professional care. Do not give pain medication until the situation has been evaluated. Elevate the affected part if it is not obviously broken and take care not to use it. Wait overnight. If the pain is severe enough to keep the patient awake much of the night, it needs to be checked by medical personnel. The ability to move an injured part, and/or the color which an injured part may become, are not indications of whether or not a bone has been broken.

~ Anaphylactic Shock ~

This can be caused by insect stings or severe food alleriges. The affected person feels faint, vomits, passes out, and can die from this. Difficulty in breathing is the primary symptom of anaphylactic shock. Hives may appear, throat may swell and wheezing may occur. If the victim has an epi-pen, administer it immediately, and call emergency services. Get immediate medical attention.

~ Croup or Whooping Cough? ~

Croup is signified by a tight, bark-like cough and shallow respirations. It may be accompanied by a fever and occasional vomiting. It rarely occurs in children over 12 years of age. It is usually viral, lasting for 3 days. Each day the symptoms are progressively better as opposed to whooping cough.

Treatment: Increase liquids. Give medication for fever as needed. Make a steam tent and have afflicted child stay in the tent as much as possible. To make a steam tent, place a sheet over a frame of some type. It could be placed over a crib. Place a cool-air vaporizor to blow into the tent. Keep as much of the vapor in the tent as possible. If respirations become close and labored and abdomen sucks in deeply with each respiration, seek medical attention.

Notes from *Mother Dear*, B.R.N.*

*B.R.N. *is a degree that can only be bestowed on Mother Dear,*
the only one qualified to be the **Beloved Resident Nurse.**

" . . .*inasmuch as ye have done it unto*
one of the least of these my brethren,
ye have done it unto me."
Matthew 25:40

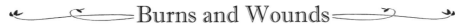

Minor Burns

1st Degree ~ Will hurt and turn red. Heals within a day or so. Treat with aloe-vera or tea-tree oil immediately. Re-apply when burn becomes uncomfortable. 2nd Degree ~ Will hurt badly and blister. Do not "pop" a blister. It is nature's best bandage and will keep infection out as long as it stays intact.

Serious Burns

Blisters and pops immediately. When placed under cold running water, top layers of skin slough off. May or may not hurt and needs to be treated by a trained medical professional.

Wounds

Wash scrapes and scratches immediately. The sooner it is washed, the less it will hurt. This is the time to aggressively get the sand and grit out, if it is ever coming out! Once it has started healing, it is too late! Next, rinse the area with soap and water twice on the first day and repeat, if necessary, on subsequent days and apply antibiotic ointment to aid in healing and to prevent infection from setting in.

Cuts

Clean well. Hold edges pinched tightly together with a strong piece of tape cut into this shape. ▯─▯
If using antibiotic ointment use this shape ▭ and do not get any where tape must stick. It simply will not stick where the ointment is. Super glue and even common white glue have at times been used successfully to hold a small cut together. Clean thoroughly first to prevent sealing in infection. If the cut is on the face, it is more likely to require a physician's attention. Scars in the whisker area can be troublesome to a man for many years. Be aware that some people produce more scar tissue than others. While a small scar may be interpreted as manly, it is never desirable on a lady. Treat these cuts prudently. Golden seal powder (an herb that aids in sealing the cut) can be sprinkled on. Keep the area clean and dry. If any sign of infection (redness, heat, pain increase, or red streak) is present, apply iodine-based solution for 5 minutes, twice a day. Removing tape before 3-5 days have passed, can cause the wound to re-open.

Puncture Wounds

Squeeze to encourage bleeding-this helps clean the wound. Saturate with an iodine-based solution twice a day. Keep area clean and apply antibiotic ointment liberally. If patient acquires a fever or the area looks infected, (see signs above), seek medical attention.

~ Natural Antibiotic ~

Garlic is a natural antibiotic. It is easy to obtain and inexpensive. A few bulbs can save a person much misery, time, and money. The property *allicin* found in garlic is very effective against many types of bacteria. Garlic can be used topically and systemically. To use topically, peel and slice a little off to get to the oil inside. Rub this oil on the infected site or cut a thin slice and tape it on the affected area. It can also be eaten raw to help with infections. Simply cut a thin slice, chew it and swallow and refrain from eating or drinking for 20 minutes.

~ Garlic Vinegar ~

Garlic vinegar can be used topically. It makes an excellent swab for sore throats and skin infections. If applied immediately after accidentally biting the inside of the cheek or tongue, the sore will heal quickly. To prepare garlic-vinegar, fill a small glass jar with thin garlic slices. Cover with apple cider vinegar and cap. Let ripen for three weeks for greatest benefit, though it can be used immediately. This concoction will remain viable for months.

~ Garlic Soup ~

Garlic can be used effectively to prevent or cure secondary infections (ear, sinus, or lung). A secondary infection is one resulting from a virus. To use garlic as a systemic antibiotic, peel and chop 6 fresh cloves. Simmer garlic in ¾ cup water for 15 minutes. Do not let boil dry ~ burnt garlic reeks! Serve with salt & pepper and a few soda crackers. Add a pinch of chicken broth powder to make it more flavorful. To obtain the healing properties of the garlic, the garlic pieces and the broth must both be consumed. For a child's dose, reduce the number of cloves to 3. This can be repeated every day as necessary, up to 3 times per day.

~ Coughs, Congestion, Minor Sore Throat ~

For congestion in the lungs, use 1 part apple cider vinegar to 4 parts water. Bring to boil. Place pot on the table. The patient closes his eyes and puts his head over the vapors, covering the head and pot with a towel to retain the steam. Breathe through nose and mouth to reduce nasal and lung congestion. This is very effective for a cough, also. Coughing is caused by swelling and/or irritation of the throat, or by something in the lungs (such as mucus). One way to reduce swelling is by elevating the person's head. Also, applying an icy-cold cloth to the throat, sucking on ice chips, or consuming frozen commodities (like a popsicle), can reduce swelling, thereby reducing the coughing. If coughing is a result of nasal drainage from allergy or virus, swab the throat with garlic~vinegar.

When swabbing, avoid touching the *uvula* which dangles in the center of the throat. It will cause a gag reflex. Swab the circular part on each side of the throat. Gargling with warm salt water or slightly diluted garlic-vinegar, every two hours, will also help heal a sore throat.

~ Vinegar Bath ~

A warm vinegar bath is helpful with yeast infections and muscle aches. It serves to pull toxins out of the body. Add 2-4 cups of apple cider vinegar to a 1/2 tub of warm water. Soak the body for half an hour or more. Can be repeated as often as necessary.

~ GoldenSeal ~

This herb acts to kill germs and makes cuts and scratches seal shut. Use on umbilical cords on a newborn and C-section incisions. This home remedy is tried and true!

~ Plantain ~

Plantain grows readily in the wild and in many backyards. Check a book from the library to know how to readily identify this helpful plant. When mashed and applied to the skin, plantain pulls toxins through the skin's surface. Use on ant bites, wasp stings, and acne.

~ Tea-tree Oil ~

This works wonders on minor burns and insect bites. See resources for 100's of other uses for this oil and where to purchase.

What is the difference between a virus and an infection? Though I went through nurses' training and had my R.N. license, when the older of my nine children were young, I was often at the Dr's office. He told me on several visits that there was nothing to be done for my sick child, just take him home and treat the symptoms, because what he had was only a virus. I finally asked the elderly doctor how I could tell if my child had a virus or an infection without bringing him into the office each time he was ill. He told me this, "If the child is feverish and lethargic, give him something for the fever. He will respond in one of two ways. If he has a virus his fever will come down within 30 minutes and he will feel like getting back to play. If he has an infection (like ears) his fever will be slower to come down and he will remain lethargic." This advice has saved me many trips to the Dr's office.

Mrs. Jan Stafford, R.N.

Family Medical History

*Record any illness or disease occurring in your
family that could possibly affect the generations to come.*

Date   Disease/Illness   Afflicted Member + Relationship

_____

_____

_____

_____

_____

_____

_____

_____

_____

_____

_____

_____

_____

_____

_____

*"Bless the Lord,
O my soul,
and forget not
all his benefits;
who forgiveth all thine
iniquities; who healeth
all thy diseases."*
Psalm 103:2-3

Resources

Puritans Pride
Call 800.645.1030 for a free catalog.
Vitamins, herbs, ointments, tea-tree oil & more.

Adventure Medical Kits
PO Box 43309, Oakland, CA 94624
800.324.3517
First-aid kits pre-packaged for travel & camping.

La-Leche League
800.525.3243
Help for new mothers and breastfeeding mothers.

Poison Control Center
Call immediately for any poisoning emergency!
800.222.1222

"Australian Tea-Tree Oil First-Aid Handbook"
Available from Kali Press
800.726.1612
101 uses for tea-tree oil

Vaccinations - Deception & Tragedy
by Michael Dye
Do not make uninformed decisions.
Hallelujah Acres Health Ministries
704.481.1700

Cascade Healthcare Supplies
1826 NW 18th Street
Portland, OR 97209
Request Catalog at 800.443.9942
Birth kits, hot water bottles, bandages, thermometers,
bulk herbs, sanitary pads, ear care products, & more.
Meeting the needs of midwives, birth centers and
families with quality healthcare products.

Use this blank page for journaling or attach snippets and clippings for keepsakes.

Gardening

Use this blank page for journaling or attach snippets and clippings for keepsakes.

"Memories are the sweetest flowers of the garden."

Use this blank page for journaling or attach snippets and clippings for keepsakes.

If you would be happy for a week — take a wife.
If you would be happy for a month — kill a pig.
But if you would be happy your whole life — plant a garden.
~ mid 17th century ~

Steps for Beginning Your Garden

Begin with a plan in mind. It would be ideal to begin working your plot in the autumn season, before the winter freeze.

Once you have selected your plot, prepare your soil by turning over the ground, either by hand or with a garden tiller. Remove all the sod by hand and place this in your compost pile.

Cover the area with a layer of old newspapers (black & white ink only), a moderate layer of rich, fertile compost, manure, chicken litter or leaves, and on top of that a sheet of black plastic. Weight down the plastic with pieces of wood or rocks. This step is not essential, but gives you a good head start by feeding your soil and killing most of the potential weeds that would sprout during planting season.

Follow the planting seasons in your area and do not plant too early as a hoary frost may devour all your sincere but hasty efforts.

Borrow books from the library on gardening and educate yourself from your readings. Many books have lovely photographs that will inspire you in your gardening ventures.

Plant in rows, blocks, or raised beds. If planting in raised beds, you will leach valuable nutrients from the soil more quickly than if you plant in rows or blocks on your plot. However, you can easily replenish the soil with homemade, fertile compost.

Consider planting complimentary plants which help repel pests and disease. Marigold, or the herbal cousin, Calendula, is wonderful for keeping all sorts of bugs away from the garden. These are easy to grow from seed. When planted in and around your garden rows, they brighten up your garden with colorful blooms, and act as an all-purpose pest deterrent.

After your seeds have sprouted and grown to be a few inches high, begin a schedule of weeding and hoeing. A bit of weeding in the garden is good therapy for the soul and body. If weeds are kept in check while they are still small, it will not be a daunting task. It is when you neglect your garden and allow it to get unsightly, that it becomes an overwhelming job.

Contributed by ~ *Mrs. Kimberly Eddy*

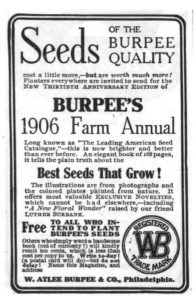

You can learn more about gardening in these upcoming books titled:

"Momma's Guide to Growing Your Own Groceries"

& "Momma's Herb Garden"

Joyful Momma Publications
PO Box 112
Fostoria, MI 48435

For years my mother-in-law sprayed her apple and pear trees, but continued to get bad fruit that appeared to be bug damaged. She finally gave up in frustration, stopped spraying the poor trees, and simply composted all of her damaged apples and pears. A few years later, as I became more proficient in gardening, my tomato plants were suffering from rotting on their bottoms. I discovered that the disease affecting them was called, "Blossom End Rot." It is caused by not enough calcium in the soil, and not being watered evenly. As I researched this problem, I realized it was essentially the same problem in my mother-in-law's trees. I learned that mottled fruit in fruit trees was not from bugs, but caused by a calcium deficiency. My mother-in-law was skeptical, but she spread calcium around her trees in the fall and again in the spring. She harvested bushels of lovely, healthy fruit that fall.

Mrs. Kimberly Eddy

Basics for the Home Vegetable Garden

Tomatoes ~ There are so many varieties available to plant: Romas, cherries, slicing tomatoes, yellow tomatoes, specialty varieties for salsa and more! If you are starting with seeds, begin indoors in flats 8 weeks before planting season. When seedlings develop 4 or more leaves and become about 3 inches tall, transplant into small individual pots. Keep well watered and give plenty of sunlight from a window. Harden by setting in a protected area outside in warmer weather for a week or so before setting them out into your garden rows. Tomatoes will need some sort of staking or wire cages to support them. If you haven't started your seeds early on, it is best to buy small plants from your local garden center or from roadside produce stands instead of directly seeding them into the garden.

Enjoy Home Grown Vegetables

Early Peas ~ These are the first thing to be planted in the garden when the weather is still cool. They can withstand a bit of frost if planted deep in a furrow for protection. Pick early, as soon as pods are filled out. If left on the vine, they will become tough and starchy. Enjoy them raw in salads and lightly steamed with butter and salt. If you have never eaten fresh, sweet garden peas, you don't know what you are missing!

Green Beans ~ There are climbing varieties and bush-type varieties. Easily grown from seed. Plant in late spring when the ground has warmed.

Pick while young and tender. These preserve well for winter by canning in glass jars using a pressure cooker.

Potatoes ~ These are free to grow in your backyard garden. You can just cut the "eyes" off the potatoes you have in your pantry. Cut chunks about 2 inches and bury them in hills about 3 inches deep. Potash will help develop the root growth, giving you larger potatoes. Keep the soil pulled over the tubers to prevent the skins from turning green. This can be toxic and causes the potato to have a bitter taste. Potato bugs will be a problem and must be controlled. Check with local gardeners as to what has worked well for them. Harvest potatoes when the leaves of the plant turn brown. Dig, dig, dig, and you will be blessed with bundles of lovely new potatoes.

Squash ~ These will need a large, wide row as the plants spread to a large size. They are easily grown from seed and only a few plants are sufficient for a family as they are well-known for being prolific. Some varieties are baked and others boiled. Yellow crookneck squash is delicious stir-fried in olive oil with garlic and onions. If you have an over-abundance of zucchini, it can be grated and frozen to make a quick bread similar to banana bread. You may even get brave enough to try some garden fresh squashes raw in your summer salads.

Cucumbers ~ This is one of the oldest cultivated plants in the world. It is even mentioned that they were eaten in Egypt in the Old Testament. The cucumber row needs to be about 3-4 feet wide. For space savers, train them to grow up a trellis. Pick fruits regularly. Leaving fruit on the vine causes the future harvests to be reduced. All sorts of varieties available for pickling or slicing. Easily grown from seeds.

Leafy Greens ~ It is delightful to plant a mixed variety of seeds for a nice blend. Several can be picked at one time and cooked for an interesting combination. Broadcast seeds over a tilled and raked bed. Lightly rake into the soil. Many varieties of greens will tolerate cold weather until continuous hard freezes occur.

Herbs

Most homes of yesteryear had a backyard garden of herbs. The homekeeper considered herbs a necessity for their flavoring properties in cooking. The homekeeper also needed them for their medicinal and healing properties for her family. After a hard day in the fields, workers looked forward to the cool, refreshing glass of mint tea. Many herbs are very easy to grow and require little care except a well-drained soil and the time it takes to cut and hang them to dry. Most retain delicious scent and flavor even when dried. What a charming effect it adds to the kitchen to have a row of bundled herbs, tied with ribbons, hanging from the rafters in a corner of the kitchen.

Mrs. Martha Greene

Basic Herbs for a Backyard Herb Garden

Basil ~ *Ocimum basilicum*
Annual

Once you have tasted it fresh, this is a must-have for the backyard garden. Many varieties grow to 24 inches tall. Pick the leaves frequently, chopping them in a food processor with a little water to make a paste and freeze in ice cube trays. When cubes are frozen, pop out of mold and store in small baggies in the freezer. All you do is take a frozen cube of basil and drop it into your favorite simmering sauce for that fresh flavor of basil!

Chives ~ *Allium tuberorosum or schoenoprasum*
Perennial

Delicate onion or garlic flavor; pretty white or pink flower heads on grass-like stalks. Cut 3 inches from base before flowering and chop fine. Dry or freeze and use to flavor and garnish soups or potatoes.

Thyme ~ *Thymus sorphyllum*
Perennial

A low-growing creeper, small and shrubby, with endless varieties that can be grown. Growing from seed is not so easy, so if you do not have a green thumb, begin with transplanting a small, potted plant into your garden. To harvest, cut off the branches, dry them, and then just zip the dried leaves off by running your fingers along the stem. Delicious flavoring for many poultry dishes.

Oregano ~ *Origanum vulgare*
Perennial

There are several different kinds of oregano available, but not all of them are of high quality. The sort of oregano most of us are familiar with is actually Greek oregano or as it is sometimes called, true oregano. Grows easily from a small purchased plant. Cut many times during the season. Hardy and easy to grow.

Calendula ~ *Calendula officinalis*
Annual

This is the cousin to the common marigold flower. Makes a wonderful herb for those who make homemade soap and other cosmetic products. Remove dried flower heads and inside you will find many seeds in each head (similar to small sticks). Save to plant again the following year. These plants repel bugs from your garden and give a lovely, constant burst of golden color throughout the summer.

Mint ~ *Mentha peperita or spicata*
Perennial

Mint is very easy to grow. In fact, some gardeners might say, "Too easy!" Mint spreads quickly throughout the garden, so you either give it room to spread or contain it in a pot. One solution is to put it in a pot and then plant the pot in the ground. There are many varieties of mint available in abounding flavors. Planting mint around the outside of your home is a beautiful and practical way to help deter ants from entering.

Echinacea ~ *Echinacea augustifolia*
Perennial

Tall, pinkish, purple, daisy-like flowers; this plant has become popular in recent years as a natural immune system builder. This herb also spreads slowly so will eventually fill in whatever area you have planted it in. Makes a nice, high background flower for your herb garden. To use for medicinal purposes, you can dry the leaves and steep for a tea or harvest and dry the root in the fall.

Lemon Balm ~ *Melissa officinalis*
Perennial

This plant looks a bit similar to mint and spreads and grows rapidly. Makes refreshing iced beverages in the summer. Leaves have a pungent lemon flavor and scent.

Rosemary ~ *Rosmarinus officinalis*
Perennial

This resembles a small cedar tree and has beautiful blooms in the cold season. Snip the branches and dry and then zip across stem to remove the rosemary leaves. Crush or use whole to flavor many dishes. Very delicious on roasted chicken. It makes a pretty ornament for the kitchen. Cut 6-inch stems of rosemary and bundle together. Wrap with some raffia around the middle and then tie tightly to hold the bundle together. Arrange a few bundles in a small basket for a delicious scent and pleasing look.

Parsley ~ *Petroselinum crispum*
Biennial

Often used as a garnish, many foods are served with chopped parsley sprinkled on top. The fresh flavor of parsley goes extremely well with fish. Parsley is part of "bouquet garni," a bundle of fresh herbs used to flavor stocks, soups, and sauces. Parsley's value as a breath-freshener comes from its high concentration of chlorophyll. Parsley grows very well in a deep, thin pot on a sunny windowsill along with a lot of water. It can take a long time to get your seed to germinate, so you must be patient with parsley. You may have better success if you soak the seeds in water overnight before planting. If you give up trying from seed, buy it as a small, potted plant and it will certainly grow amazingly fast. It usually reseeds itself, so you will have a nice patch of parsley to snip. Use in your dishes for a pleasing, mild flavor and pretty, green color.

Garlic ~ *Allium sativum*
Annual

To plant garlic, break apart a head of garlic and plant each individual clove. Each clove will be one head of garlic by late summer. For best results, garlic can be planted in the autumn after the garden beds have been cleared for winter.

103

Planting Records

~ Flowers ~ Seeds ~ Bushes ~ Trees ~
I delight in all of these!

Date	Seed /Plant	Origin	Notes

Date	Seed/Plant	Origin	Notes

". . .a time to plant and a time to pluck
up that which is planted."
Ecclesiastes 3:2b

Garden Sketches

Backyard Vegetable Garden Plan
~ Sketched by Mrs. Martha Greene

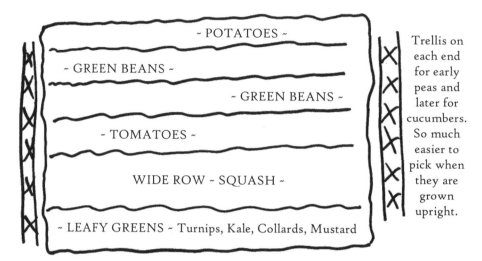

- POTATOES -

~ GREEN BEANS ~

~ GREEN BEANS ~

~ TOMATOES ~

WIDE ROW ~ SQUASH ~

~ LEAFY GREENS ~ Turnips, Kale, Collards, Mustard

Trellis on each end for early peas and later for cucumbers. So much easier to pick when they are grown upright.

Many approach pest and disease control in their gardens with a shotgun method. This is equivalent to taking every pill in your medicine cabinet to prevent illness. In essence, it often does not work. A better approach would be to observe the situation in your garden, taking note of bugs or diseases that appear to be causing damage to plants, and looking into ways of safely ridding your garden of them. Many times the solution is easier than you might think. One year, my husband gave our children a proposition. One penny for every potato bug brought to him in a capped jar. It is amazing how fast a bunch of youngsters can collect them. We had bug-free potato plants that year — they earned about $5.00 each!

Grandmother's Flower Garden Sketch

~ Sketched by Mrs. Martha Greene

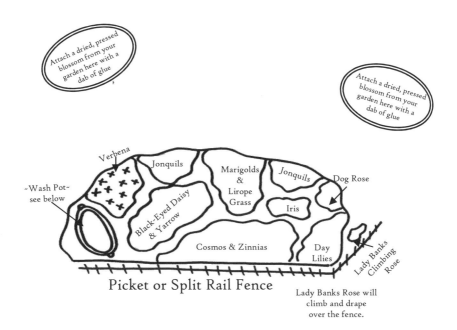

Attach a dried, pressed blossom from your garden here with a dab of glue

Attach a dried, pressed blossom from your garden here with a dab of glue

Verbena
Jonquils
Marigolds & Liriope Grass
Jonquils
Dog Rose
~Wash Pot~ see below
Black-Eyed Daisy & Yarrow
Iris
Cosmos & Zinnias
Day Lilies
Lady Banks Climbing Rose

Picket or Split Rail Fence

Lady Banks Rose will climb and drape over the fence.

To help your garden soil get healthy and stay healthy, you can use homemade compost as both a mulch and a fertilizer. As a fertilizer, dig a few inches of compost into your garden beds each fall and spring. To use as a mulch, place generous mounds of compost around established plants. It helps prevent weeds, locks in moisture for the plants and keeps the ground warm.

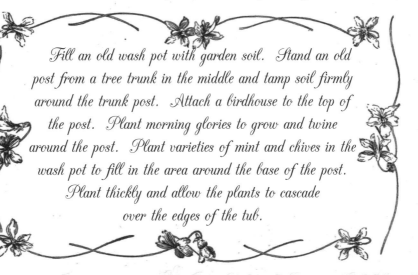

Fill an old wash pot with garden soil. Stand an old post from a tree trunk in the middle and tamp soil firmly around the trunk post. Attach a birdhouse to the top of the post. Plant morning glories to grow and twine around the post. Plant varieties of mint and chives in the wash pot to fill in the area around the base of the post. Plant thickly and allow the plants to cascade over the edges of the tub.

Backyard Herb Garden Sketch
~ Sketched by Mrs. Martha Greene

Herbs are easy to grow and require little tending. They will give you a delightful gardening experience. Their sweet aroma and variety of flavors will delight you. You will have new adventures in culinary arts using fresh herbs from your very own garden!

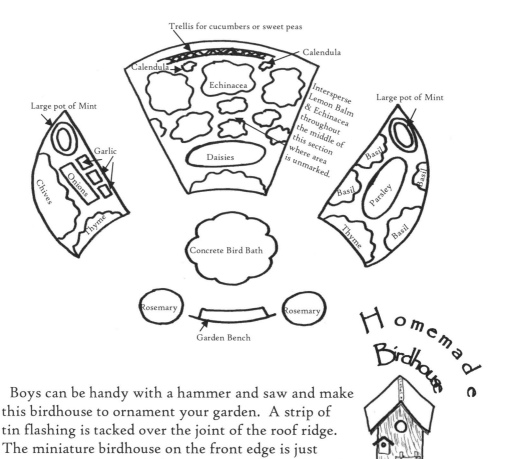

Boys can be handy with a hammer and saw and make this birdhouse to ornament your garden. A strip of tin flashing is tacked over the joint of the roof ridge. The miniature birdhouse on the front edge is just ornamental and is made from a small square of wood tacked to the front board of the house. The decorative wood fence is made from small strips of wood or straight twigs and tacked on with small tacks. The house could be painted or left as natural wood. The miniature house on the front shows up best if it contrasts with the color of the house front. An appealing look is a dark green painted birdhouse and a white roof, natural twig fence and red miniature bird house front.

Saving Seeds

Save a seed and the blooms could
be enjoyed by your children's grandchildren!

You can save any seeds from your own garden if the varieties are open-pollinated, meaning they are not hybrids or have not been crossed with other varieties in the same species. It is simple to do. Just let a few of the plants in your garden go to seed. Harvest them by picking and letting the seed pods dry in a paper sack. Once thoroughly dry, you can extract the seeds from the pods and package them in small envelopes. Be sure to label the envelopes. I keep a small basket of these on my shelf. You can also store them in the freezer. One small, dried flower head of Marigold can produce hundreds of seeds. Much less expensive than buying a packet at the garden center with only 25 seeds per package! Save seeds from watermelons, cucumbers, peppers, and tomatoes by opening the fruit, removing the seeds, and letting them dry completely on an absorbent cloth or paper towel. Package and label as stated above.

Seeds that have been saved from hybrid plants will not have the same excellent qualities as the parent plant and often will not germinate. Search for seeds in the seed catalogs that are labeled as open-pollinated or heirloom seeds. For years, I had a lovely bed of periwinkles from the seed pods saved from my grandfather's yard. Learn to save your seeds for next year's garden, and the next, and the next . . . .

Seed Saver's Exchange
3094 North Winn Road
Decorah, Iowa 52101
563.382.5990

Tip ~ Paint the handles of your garden tools with brightly-colored enamel paint like lettuce green, pansy purple, radish red and pumpkin orange. They will never get lost against the backdrop of brown dirt again, as they will be easily spotted anywhere in the garden or yard!

Old-Fashioned Flowers
for the Garden

> A = *Annual*
> Dies out after one season of producing flowers.
> B = *Biennial*
> Flowers in the second year.
> P = *Perennial*
> Produces flowers and seeds year after year without replanting.

Climbing

Morning Glory ~ *Ipomoea* ~ A ~ Easy; abundant color for a vertical arbor, fence, or trellis in an easy-to-grow vine. Twines and clings without tying. No fuss in poor soil.

Short Plants

Petunias ~ *Petunia x hybrida* ~ A ~ Blooms early summer to frost and will adapt to baskets, pots, or beds. Masses of ruffled, colored blooms to cheer you all summer.

Marigold ~ *Tagestes Patula* ~ A ~ So easy to grow even in dry, poor soil. Blooms abundantly and gives carefree color to the garden. Repels nematodes in the vegetable garden. Deadhead (remove brown, dead blossoms) to prolong flowering. Save dried flower heads for seed to plant next year.

Periwinkle ~ *Vinca rosea* ~ A ~ Blooms luxuriously from early summer to frost despite heat or drought. Constant color for your flower garden. Some varieties reseed themselves.

Verbena ~ *Verbena Bonariensis* ~ A ~ Deep lilac flower clusters have a slender branching habit that weave their way gracefully through your garden beds. Very hardy and carefree and most often reappears the next year even though it is considered an annual.

Tall Plants

Yarrow ~ *Achillea millefolium* ~ P ~ Cluster blooms in the summer with full sun, flourishing in heat, drought, and poor soil. Lovely fern like leaves. Attracts honeybees.

Black-Eyed Daisies ~ *Rudbeckia fulgidam* ~ P ~ Tall plants covered with bright, golden, daisy-like flowers with large, black centers. Masses of color on long, sturdy stems for cutting. Blooms mid-summer. Plants grow up to 24" tall.

Cosmos ~ *Cosmos bipinnatus* ~ A ~ Heat and pest-resistant. Blooms cover plants until fall frost. Easy to grow from seed. Lovely cut flowers for bouquets to brighten your home all summer.

Zinnias ~ *Zinnia elegans* ~ A ~ Blooms heavily all summer. Direct sow when soil is warmed. Has thick, sturdy stems for cut flowers. Save seeds from dried flower heads to plant in next year's garden.

Hollyhocks ~ *Althaea* ~ B ~ Full of old-fashioned warmth. Lovely in groups in the rear of the garden. Grows up to 4 feet tall. They easily re-seed themselves. Tolerates drought and thrives in full sun. Blooms by mid-summer the second year.

Roses

Dog Rose ~ *Rosa Canina* ~ P ~ No old-fashioned garden is complete without a Dog Rose! These roses do not form the large, tight buds we commonly think of as roses. Instead, they produce a smaller, open flower with a heady fragrance. They tend to be very prickly with more thorns than the modern hybrid roses. They produce tart fruits, known as Rose Hips, and are popular for their high content of Vitamin C. Can be used dried in tea.

Lady Banks Climbing Rose ~ *Rosa Banksiae Lutea* ~ P ~ An old-fashioned favorite climber rose introduced from China in the early 19th century. Forms 1-inch double-yellow flowers. This variety has thornless canes and blooms in early spring. Beautiful for arbors and fences.

Bulbs

Jonquils ~ *Narcissus Pseudonarcissus* ~ P ~ Hardy spring-flowering bulbs. Favorite flower to announce spring's arrival! Plant bulbs in late fall and mulch over for protection from winter weather.

Iris ~ *Iris Atropurpurea* ~ P ~ Actually, this is a perennial herb that grows from a rhizome, or bulb. Long, erect, flowering stems and sword-shaped leaves that grow in dense clumps. To propagate, dig rhizomes in the fall and divide, replanting each one separately. Many varieties are available in dazzling colors.

Day Lily ~ *Hemerocallis* ~ P ~ Sun with light shade. Ultra hardy, propagate by dividing bulbs. Long blooming and easy to grow.

Harvest Bounty

Orchard fruits are ripe and sweet; there is golden honey in the combs. Fields of grain are copper bright! Wild grapes hang in clusters glowing purple in the sun. Mister Frost will soon blanket our meadow. We have harvested our bounty and give thanks to the Lord above.

∼ Mrs. Martha Greene

Tomatoes

Can or freeze. For large amounts of tomatoes you don't have time to work up, you can place the washed (pat dry) tomatoes on a baking sheet. Freeze whole. When frozen through, place in plastic bags. Run under hot water and skins will peel off quickly. Use as whole tomatoes in your favorite sauce or puree them in the blender. Use the waterbath method when canning in glass jars.

Green Peppers

Wash, seed, and cut in dices. Fill small freezer bags with diced, sweet green peppers and freeze. No other processing necessary. When needed in a recipe, just choose a few from the bag and drop into your recipe. No need to thaw. If you need to thaw, just run under warm running water.

Strawberries

Wash and stem and pat dry carefully. Lay out on a baking sheet and place in freezer. As soon as berries have frozen firm, put into a self-seal freezer bag. Berries will be ready to use in smoothies.

Garlic

Dry in the sun a few days. Store in mesh bags or make garlic braids.

How to Make a Garlic Braid
12 page brochure by Diane Trenhaile
Nichol's Garden Nursery ◊ 800.422.3985

Grapes ~ Blackberries ~ Plums

Eat fresh or make preserves. During the winter months, it will delight you to have a jar of homemade preserves to serve with thick slices of homemade bread and steaming bowls of hearty stew.

Sweet Corn

Eat fresh and freeze your bounty. Freezing corn gives it a more superior taste than canning corn. It also makes efficient use of energy as it takes quite some time to process canned corn in the pressure cooker.

*"Mary, Mary, kind and heeding,
How does your garden grow?
With herbs, beans, leafy greens,
And little buds all in a row."*

Nichol's Garden Nursery
800.422.3985
1190 Old Salem Road NE
Albany, OR 97321-4580
Tools, Books, Seeds, Herbs, Bulbs

Geo. W. Park Seed Co. Inc.
800.845.3369
1 Parkton Avenue
Greenwood, SC 29647-0001
Dependable since 1868

Burgess Seed & Plant Co.
309.662.7761
905 Four Seasons Road
Bloomington, IL 61701
Good prices; Free gifts w/order

Gardens Alive
513.354.1483
5100 Schenley Place
Lawrenceburg, IN 47025
Organic Gardening Supplies

Peaceful Valley Farm Supply
530.272.4769
110 Spring Hill Drive
Grass Valley, CA 95945
Flowering Trees, Shade Trees

Johnny's Selected Seeds
207.861.3900
955 Benton Avenue
Winslow, ME 04901
Garden Tools, Culinary & Medicinal
Herb Seeds

Wayside Gardens
800.213.0379
1 Garden Lane
Hodges, SC 29695
Free Catalog, Perennials, Roses

Aunt Martha's Garden
731 E. Valley Road
Willits, CA 95490
Free Catalog, Heirloom Seed Saver's
Guide, Heirloom Seeds

Gardener's Supply Co.
800.876.5520
128 Intervale Road
Burlington, VT 05401
Pest Control, Garden Furniture, Fast
Friendly Service, Pots & Planters

Use this blank page for journaling or attach snippets and clippings for keepsakes.

Cooking
&
Baking

Use this blank page for journaling or attach snippets and clippings for keepsakes.

*"Many a bachelor longs for a wife who
would cook for him. . .
and so does many a husband!"*

119

Use this blank page for journaling or attach snippets and clippings for keepsakes.

Meal Times

Eating together serves two purposes. First, to refuel our physical bodies. Psalm 103:5 "He satisfieth thy mouth with good things; so that thy youth is renewed like the eagle's." Second, we are to fellowship while we are gathered round the table. In Deuteronomy 26:11 we see the command "to rejoice in every good thing" not only as individuals, but together as families ("thine house!") and to show hospitality to others ("the Levite and the stranger") that God may send our way.

Surveys today indicate that many people on most days eat take-out or fast-food, and often they eat their meals on the go. Cars are referred to as "mobile dining rooms." What a sad commentary on our times!

Eating together as a family is important. You are not "wasting your time" when you are sitting down and eating together as a family; you are creating a memory for your children and your husband. Consider your family schedule and work out the best time to have dinner each night. Pare down the schedule to make it fit. Show your family they are a priority by *planning* on dinner together, rather than eating together only when it happens to be convenient.

Is your meal table unpleasant and stressful? Is there an atmosphere of arguing and bickering? Is the food unappetizing? That would be difficult for anyone to want to sit at and enjoy. Determine to make your table a pleasant place that your family loves and enjoys. Before your husband comes home, pray for your home to be a peaceful haven for him. Then, tidy up the dining area and don't forget to fix your hair and freshen up! Learn to season the food well so it looks, smells, and tastes wonderful. Train the children during other parts of the day in proper table manners and what you will expect of them. Find out what your husband likes and then fix it! Some men love meat and potatoes, some love salads, and some could care less. Some are fussy and some are not. Some husbands appreciate a lovely table, while others don't notice a thing unless their chair is sticky with jelly. Find out what pleases your husband and seek to honor him by doing it.

Adapted from ~

Joyful Momma Publications
POB 112 ~ Fostoria, Michigan 48435
Used with permission

The Pantry

A pantry is a small closet or room off the kitchen, reserved as a place for your food stores, conveniently lined with storage shelves. Many homes may not be arranged with this addition, so another large cupboard will have to do. A homekeeper living in small quarters may have to be creative with solutions as to where to store her food goods. Remember that sunlight may destroy vitamin content or work to cause deterioration of flavors, and heat and moisture encourage the growth of molds and bacteria. It is imperative, no matter your living arrangement, that you find a cool, dry, dark place for your food storage. Remember to place new food goods toward the back of the shelves, so the older items are used first.

Staple Foods for Your Kitchen Pantry Stores
(which would include your cupboards, freezer and refrigerator)

FRUITS: fresh, dried, canned

MEATS & FISH: canned, frozen

BEVERAGES: coffee, cocoa, tea, dry mixes, frozen concentrate, vegetable juices, fruit juices

CEREALS & GRAINS: rice, pastas, corn meal, oatmeal, boxed breakfast, granola, whole grains, grits

CHEESES: sliced, block, cottage cheese

BREADS: loaf, rolls, buns, crackers

COCONUT: frozen, dried

OILS: butter, cooking oils, vegetable shortening

SUGAR: brown, confectioner's, white granulated, sugar-substitutes

FLOURS: whole grain, all-purpose, self-rising, specialty bread flour

ONIONS: green, chives, yellow, red

POTATOES: white, red, yams, frozen fries

SYRUPS: molasses, corn syrup, honey, maple, fruit syrups

DRESSINGS: mayonnaise, mustard, salad dressing, vinaigrette, ketchup

EGGS: fresh white or brown, egg substitutes

MILKS: cream, canned evaporated, condensed, buttermilk, dry powder

JAMS: jellies, fruit preserves

NUTS: whole, slivered, nut butters

SEASONINGS: chicken, beef, vegetable bouillon cubes, seasoned salt

VEGETABLES: fresh, canned, frozen

SOUP: canned, dry packet mixes

SAUCES: hot pepper, steak sauce, Worcestershire™, soy sauce

GELATINS: flavored, unflavored, instant pudding
DRIED BEANS: pinto, navy, kidney, black turtle, lentils
THICKENERS: cornstarch, arrowroot, tapioca
FLAVORINGS: vanilla, butter, almond, maple, coconut, lemon
LEAVENING: baking soda, baking powder, yeast
SPICES: ground & stick cinnamon, ground & whole cloves,
    ground ginger, allspice, nutmeg, bay leaves, sea salt, peppercorns,
    celery seed, celery salt, dry mustard, paprika, chili powder, cayenne,
    curry powder, garlic salt and onion salt, minced garlic, basil, sage,
    tarragon, marjoram, rosemary, cumin, fennel seed, turmeric.

Pests in the Pantry?

Get the Pantry Trap for flying moth pests—It works! Have you ever seen any little brown moths flitting about in your cupboards? A mass of fine webs clinging inside a box of pasta? These are called "flour moths" and are a real nuisance if not terminated! Purchase Cupboard Moth Traps. They are non-toxic and free of pesticides. One trap lasts for 12 weeks and works by both scent and sight to catch the moths. Use them in cupboards or the pantry to eliminate food-attacking moths.

Gardens Alive
5100 Schenley Place
Lawrencebrug, IN 47025
513.354.1483

Kitchen Tools

There is always work to do in the kitchen and your assistants (kitchen tools) make the tasks so much easier! Quality kitchen tools are a wise investment. Shop for them, buying the best you can afford. There is a wide variety of modern conveniences to be found for the cook. Purchase the basics and avoid a multitude of needless gadgets that will only add clutter to your kitchen.

Essentials for the Kitchen

Basics for Stove-top Cooking:
Frying pan or skillet in two sizes
Saucepans in three sizes
One large, deep pot for soups and stews
Tea kettle for heating water

Basics for Oven Baking:
Baking sheets
Oven-proof casserole dishes
Pie pans
Square cake pans
Loaf pans

Muffin pan
Round cake pans
Wire cooling rack
9"x 13" baking pan
Roaster pan

Basic Utensils:
Paring, serrated & bread knives
Pizza cutter
Pastry roller or rolling pin
Biscuit cutter
Measuring cups & spoon set
Can opener
Ice-cream scoop
Wooden mixing spoons
Vegetable peeler
Pastry blender

Oven mitt & hot pads
Kitchen scissors
Spatula
Tongs
Turning fork
Pie server
Pancake turner
Slotted spoon
Mixing bowls in assorted sizes
Wire whisk

Basic Kitchen Equipment:
Electric beater
Crockpot
Electric Blender
Toaster
Coffeemaker

Electric or stove-top griddle
Electric skillet
Waffle iron
Large kitchen mixer
Timer

In the Kitchen

Ever wished you were blessed with a "born knack for baking"? Stop your wishing! There's no such thing to be had! Baking is a skill made and not born. Cooking is an art to be learned. It takes no special gift, no magic touch, to work wonders with a mixing bowl. Some old-fashioned cooks seemed to toss things together and achieved glorious results. Their secret was long practice! Doing a job over and over gives one a sense of how it should look and feel. Whether you are a beginner or an old hand at cooking and baking, follow these simple basic rules for wonderful results.

The family table should be simply but correctly set.

The food should be attractively served.

Good table manners should be practiced at every meal.

1 ~ Be orderly. Do your planning before you start. Choose your recipe, read it through carefully, understand it clearly. Collect all the ingredients it calls for in their order; assemble all the utensils you will need on your work table. It makes the job a joy, and it saves you time, money, and many a worried moment in your baking.

2 ~ Always wash your hands with warm water and soap before you handle food, set the table, or begin to cook. Dry them on a clean towel.

3 ~ Use good tools. Good tools simplify baking. They enable you to do things more easily and more accurately.

4 ~ Choose good ingredients. You can't do first-rate baking and cooking with second-rate ingredients. Be sure they are fresh and of the finest quality.

5 ~ Measure accurately. That is a baking "must." The finest ingredients or the greatest skill in mixing cannot overcome mistakes in the amount of ingredients. All measurements are level unless specified differently in the recipe.

6 ~ Wipe up spills and splatters on counters or floors immediately.

7 ~ Keep the working area clean, washing soiled dishes and utensils as you work. Working in the kitchen is more pleasurable when it is tidy.

8 ~ Know what to do in case of a fire. Never put water onto a grease fire! Use salt or baking soda to smother.

9 ~ Turn handles of pots and pans on the stovetop inward to prevent them being in the line of traffic and being accidentally knocked off.

10 ~ Avoid steam burns: Remove lids from hot pots by lifting the far side first, allowing steam to rise away from you and your hands.

~ portions adapted from "All About Home Baking," ©1933

Menu Patterns

Morning Meal
Fruit or Fruit Juice
Cereals, Milk or Milk Substitute
Bread with Spreads
Beverage

Light Meal
Salad or Raw Vegetables
Sandwich or Soup
Beverage

Main Meal
Meat or Meat Alternative
Potatoes, Pasta or Rice
Cooked Vegetable
Raw Salad
Bread & Butter
Beverage

Well-Planned Menus

A menu is a list of food served at a meal, but you will need a meal pattern as a guide (see page 126) to help you plan that meal. Decide on the main dish and then build a meal around that food. Choose foods that are in season; they will be lower in price. Try to have some meat, eggs, cheese, or dried beans at each meal for protein. Besides being nutritious, your meal will need to appeal to the taste and look inviting, too. Menus will be varied depending on these factors:

~ family likes or dislikes ~
~ food budget ~
~ skill and experience of the cook ~
~ time allowed for preparing the food ~
~ size of family and the member's ages ~
~ cooking facilities at hand ~
~ geographic location ~
~ season of the year ~

Tips for Planning the Menu

- Serve the food at the right temperature: cold foods cold; hot foods hot.
- To add interest, combine different sizes and shapes of food in your menu.
- Contrast the food textures. Have neither all hard and crispy foods, nor all soft foods.
- Vary your colors! How would a plate of white navy beans, creamy mashed potatoes, stewed turnips, and applesauce go over? Make the plate look inviting with a slice of red tomato or a crispy green pickle.
- Compliment flavors of the foods on your menu. Contrast strong flavors with mild, and some sweet with sour. Be creative and add a little extra to the menu than what is expected. A homemade muffin is a welcome treat with a dish of hearty soup!
- Plan a week of tentative menus for snacks and meals. This will help avoid repetition and give you a chance to serve a variety of foods.
- The meals and snacks served during the course of the day should build on each other and give your family the optimum nutrition they need to grow and thrive.

Measuring

When her cake failed, or her biscuits turned out sadly, the old-fashioned housewife sighed and said, "Bad luck"! However, the chances are that it wasn't her luck that was wrong; it was her measuring. In those days, you see, her recipes were handed down from mother to daughter, with such measurements as "enough flour to make a nice stiffness" . . ."butter the size of an egg" . . ."a generous goblet of sugar" . . .as much saleratus /baking soda/ as will lie on a penny." And when daughter's cake couldn't quite hold a candle to mother's, it very likely was because her idea of a "nice stiffness" or "the size of an egg" was different from mother's. How exactly do you measure a generous goblet of sugar and is "butter the size of an egg" to be the size of a large egg or a small one? Today, it is a happier story. Recipes travel all over the land, and thanks to the efforts of food experts, they all talk one language. It is a language that enables you to achieve correct measurements every time~ standard measurements.

Always use standard measurements. A standard measuring cup (the equivalent of 16 tablespoons) is grooved on the side to read ¼, ½, and ¾. Standard measuring spoons include 1 tablespoon, 1 teaspoon, ½ teaspoon and ¼ teaspoon. Measurements are always level measurements.

Practical Weights and Measures

4 ounces	¼ pound
16 ounces	1 pound
60 drops	1 teaspoon
3 teaspoons	1 tablespoon
4 tablespoons	¼ cup
8 tablespoons	½ cup
16 tablespoons	1 cup
2 cups	1 pint
4 cups	2 pints or 1 quart
A dash	less than one-eighth teaspoon

"A pint's a pound, the world around."

The Butcher, the Baker, the Happy Homemaker

Pressed Pie Pastry

In a mixing bowl, combine with a fork:
1 ¾ cup unbleached, all-purpose flour
¼ teaspoon salt
½ cup + 2 tablespoons corn oil
2 tablespoons ice cold water
Press into a pie plate with fingertips. Press evenly from center out to edges until about one-eighth inch thick. Trim off
excess around edges leaving enough to pinch an edge. To bake pie shell, place in hot oven, 425°, for 12 to 15 minutes.
Makes one 10" crust.

*If you never cook in your kitchen,
it will always stay clean!
Be thankful for dirty dishes. It means
you've enjoyed a home-cooked meal.*

Best Basic Muffins

Combine in a mixing bowl:
1 ¾ cups unbleached all-purpose flour
2 tablespoons sugar
¾ teaspoon salt
2 ½ teaspoons baking powder
Make a well in the center and add in:
1 egg, beaten
¾ cup milk
¼ cup + 2 tablespoons cooking oil
Stir only until flour is incorporated. Spoon batter into paper-lined muffin pans. Fill ¾ full. Bake for 25 minutes at 400°.
Serve warm with butter and jam.
Yield: 1 dozen muffins.

Basic Buttermilk Biscuits

Mix together in a mixing bowl:
2 cups unbleached, all-purpose flour
¾ teaspoon salt
3 teaspoons baking powder
1 teaspoon baking soda
Cut in with a fork or pastry blender:
4 tablespoons vegetable shortening
Mixture should resemble coarse crumbs.
Add in to make a soft dough:
1 cup buttermilk
Gather together and knead lightly two or three times. Roll or pat out on
a floured surface to one-half inch thickness. Cut out with a biscuit cutter
and place biscuits on a greased baking sheet.
Bake for 13-15 minutes at 425° on top rack of the oven.
Makes 12-15 biscuits.

Basic Griddle Cakes

Place all ingredients in a mixing bowl and beat until
smooth with a wire whisk:
1 ½ cups unbleached, all-purpose flour
1 cup whole wheat flour
2 tablespoons baking powder
2 tablespoons sugar
1 teaspoon salt
2 eggs
4 tablespoons cooking oil
2 cups milk
Cook on hot griddle, turning only once when one side bubbles.
Serve hot with butter and maple syrup.
Makes 14-16 griddle cakes.

Basic Plain Cake

Beat all ingredients together in a mixing bowl:
2 ½ cups self-rising flour
1 ½ cups vegetable oil
4 eggs
2 cups sugar
1 cup buttermilk
1 teaspoon vinegar
1 teaspoon vanilla
Pour into a greased and lightly floured 9"x 13" pan.
Bake for 40-45 minutes at 350°.
Frost when completely cooled.

Basic Icing

½ cup soft butter
4 cups confectioner's sugar, sifted to remove lumps
4 tablespoons milk
1 tsp. flavoring (vanilla, butter, lemon, etc.)
Beat with electric beaters until smooth and fluffy. If frosting seems too
thick, add in extra milk (½ teaspoon at a time) until it is of spreading
consistency. Yields enough to frost one 9"x 13" cake
or an 8" two-layer cake.

Basic Oatmeal Cookies

Place in the large bowl of your kitchen mixer:
½ cup vegetable shortening
½ cup brown sugar
Cream together and then add in:
1 cup rolled oats
½ cup dry milk powder
¼ cup water
1 ¼ cups flour
1 ½ teaspoons baking powder
½ teaspoon salt
Mix well and then drop by teaspoonfuls (for giant-size cookies, use an ice
cream scoop) onto a greased baking sheet. Bake for 13-15 minutes at 325°.
Remove from oven; let cookies stand on baking sheet for 5 minutes and
then place on wire racks to cool completely.

Steamed White Rice

Combine in a heavy saucepan:
1 cup rice (long grain, white)
2 cups water
½ teaspoon salt (optional)
Bring to a boil over medium high heat. Cover and reduce to a simmer.
Do not stir or lift the lid for 15 minutes. After cooking time has elapsed,
turn off heat source and let stand covered until ready to serve. Fluff with
a fork before serving.

Oven Baked Brown Rice

Place in a 2-quart glass oven-proof dish with tight-fitting lid:
1 cup brown rice
2 ½ cups water
½ teaspoon salt
1 tablespoon butter or olive oil
Cover dish and bake at 400° for 1 hour and 15 minutes or until all liquid
has been absorbed. Let stand in warm oven until ready to serve.

Seasoned Yellow Rice

1 cup white long-grain rice, not instant or quick-cook
2 chicken bouillon cubes
¼ teaspoon turmeric (adds yellow color)
¼ teaspoon salt
2 cups chicken broth
3 tablespoons butter
Place all ingredients in a heavy saucepan and cover. Cook covered on
medium heat for 20 minutes. Turn off heat source and let stand covered
for 10 minutes. Fluff with a fork and serve hot.

Cutting a Whole Chicken

Step 1 ~ Wash with clear, cold water, rubbing lightly.

Step 2 ~ Cut through the skin and joint, cutting the wing from the body. Do this for both wings. Clip off wing tips at second joint. Discard.

Step 3 ~ Cut off the legs. Press outward and downward and you will disengage the hip joint from the body. Using a sharp knife, cut a large gash though the skin until you sever the leg from the body. Use whole for leg quarters or cut through knee joint of leg and thigh to make 2 pieces.

Step 4 ~ Separate the body into two pieces by cutting apart the breast from the back. See Fig. A for cutting line.

Step 5 ~ Cut breast into 2 pieces by slicing through heavy cartiledge down the center (lengthwise) of the breast.

Step 6 ~ Rinse pieces and pat dry. Proceed with cooking.

Fig. A

Country Fried Chicken

Rinse chicken pieces and pat dry with a paper towel. Place chicken pieces in a small bowl of buttermilk. Remove pieces 2 at a time, shaking off excess buttermilk. Place in a small brown paper sack:
1 cup flour
2 teaspoons seasoned salt
1 teaspoon black pepper
Put 2 pieces of chicken in at a time, shaking to coat.
Heat vegetable oil in a heavy skillet to medium high heat. Brown chicken slowly, with skillet uncovered. When one side is brown, turn over and cover skillet partially, leaving room for steam to escape. Brown on other side on medium low heat. Drain on paper towels to remove excess grease. Serve hot or cold.

Easy Baked Pork Chops

Combine in a shallow bowl:
1 cup coarse cracker crumbs
3 tablespoons Parmesan cheese
1 teaspoon black pepper
1 teaspoon seasoned salt
Combine in a small bowl:
1 egg, beaten
2 tablespoons milk
Melt 4 tablespoons of butter in a baking dish. Take 6 boneless pork chops and dip into crumb mixture. Then dip into egg mixture and once again into crumbs. Lay coated chops into butter in the baking dish. Bake for 30 minutes at 325°. Turn chops over and bake for 30 minutes longer.

"To market, to market to buy a fat pig!
Home again, home again, jiggity, jig!"

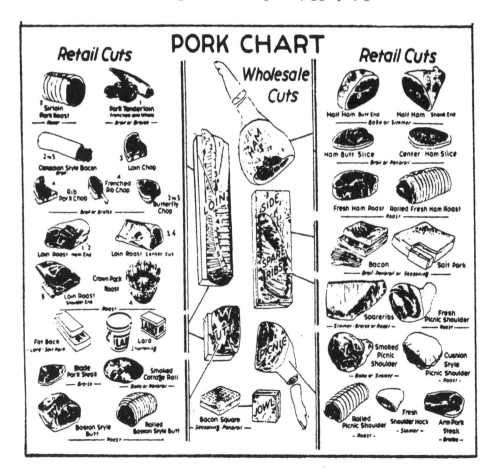

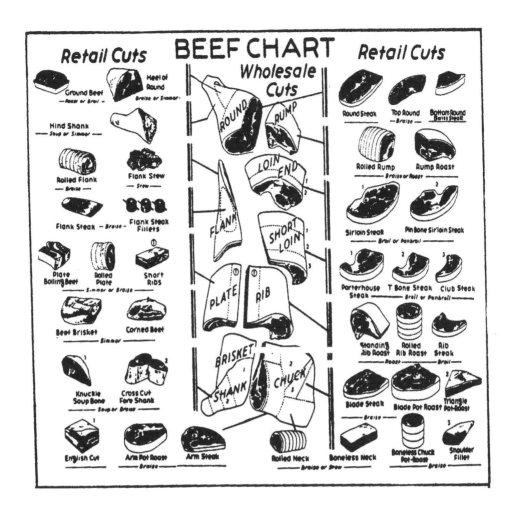

Barbequed Beef Buns

In a heavy saucepan, brown 3 pounds of lean ground beef.
Drain off excess fat and add in:
1 onion, chopped
½ cup beef broth (use 1 bouillon cube and water)
½ cup ketchup
3 tablespoons vinegar
1 tablespoon mustard
3 tablespoons brown sugar
¼ cup chopped celery
Simmer slowly for 1 hour. Place spoonfuls on large sandwich buns. Top
with a slice of cheese and place bun pieces together. Serve warm. Beef
sandwich filling may be frozen for convenient quick-fix meals.

Meat Gravy

For 1 cup gravy: 2 tablespoons fat; 2 tablespoons flour; 1 cup liquid
For 4 cups gravy: 8 tablespoons fat; 8 tablespoons flour; 4 cups liquid

When meat is cooked, remove it from the skillet or roaster pan.
Tip pan to let drippings flow into the corner. Pour drippings into a separate bowl, leaving brown bits in the pan to give richness and flavor to your gravy. Set aside bowl of drippings to let fat rise up to the top.

Pour ¾ cup water into the pan or skillet and simmer. Scrape and stir this brown liquid to loosen the browned bits that add to the flavor. Pour this browned liquid into a separate small bowl.

Skim off fat from drippings and measure out the portion needed to make your gravy. (See measurements above for 1 cup or 4 cups or adjust to amount of gravy you need to make.) Place in a skillet and heat on low heat. Add in flour (see measurements above), stirring until mixture is smooth and lightly browned. Remove pan from heat.

Measure out browned liquid and fat-skimmed drippings (see measurement above) and add slowly into browned flour mixture, stirring constantly. Cook slowly on medium heat until bubbly and thickened. Season with salt and pepper. Serve piping hot in a gravy boat.

Basic White Sauce

Melt in a small saucepan:
2 tablespoons butter
Stir in:
2 tablespoons flour
1 cup milk
Stir quickly with a wire whisk to remove lumps and then add in:
1 more cup milk
Cook for 1 minute, stirring constantly. Add in salt and pepper to taste.
A variety of seasonings or ingredients can be added to this to make
flavored sauces (i.e., mushrooms, onions, cheese, celery,
parsley, chicken or beef bouillon, etc.)

Family Recipes

Every homekeeper has her own recipes for favorite foods and family traditions. Record your family recipes here, including who it was from and when you like to serve it. Have loved ones handcopy onto some of these pages some of their favorites. A handwritten recipe will become a treasured keepsake over the passage of time.

138

Use this blank page for journaling or attach snippets and clippings for keepsakes.

Reserves
for the
Family

Use this blank page for journaling or attach snippets and clippings for keepsakes.

" *What are you preserving in your memory jar,*
as food for your restless soul,
when the winter of life comes?"

Use this blank page for journaling or attach snippets and clippings for keepsakes.

Preparing for Emergency

Emergencies such as earthquakes, blizzards, fires, tornados, floods or hurricanes will occur. In emergency situations like these you need to be prepared for your family to "weather" the initial 72 hours as that is the elapse time required before Federal Disaster Relief will be mobilized. It would be wise as a homekeeper to have a "72-Hour Emergency Kit" prepared and stored in an accessible place. The kit is primarily composed of water, food which does not require refrigeration or cooking, first-aid items, and other essentials. Kits can be as simple or sophisticated as your budget and imagination will allow you to make them. The items in your kit should be easily carried in one or two containers and ready at a moment's notice. Water is the most important commodity. The minimum required is 2 quarts, with up to 2 gallons needed per day per person. This would be for drinking, cooking, and hand washing.

Tips on Storing Water

2-liter soda drink bottles can be rinsed and used to store water for emergencies. The soda pop bottles are thick plastic so odor and taste are not readily transferred. Fill each clean 2 liter bottle with water and add in 8 drops of chorine bleach to keep the water pure for extended periods.

Essentials for a 72-Hour Emergency Kit

___flashlight
___batteries
___first-aid kit
___ready-to-eat foods
___water-proof ponchos
___water-proof matches
___candles
___tri-fold shovel
___basic tools
___bar soap
___toothbrushes
___rope
___emergency blankets

Contributed by ~ *Mrs. Marilyn Moll*

EMERGENCY ESSENTIALS ~ 800.999.163
Resource for emergency tools, freeze-dried foods,
emergency lighting, food storage containers.

147

This is a list of items to be gathered if you are aware that an emergency is pending. Do not wait until these items would be scarce. You must prepare in advance. Large garbage cans on wheels are great for long-term storage. Make sure they have tight-fitting lids. Keep food items in a separate container for ease of rotation over long periods of storage. Filled cans can be kept handily stored in a back corner of the garage. ✍ *Mrs. Martha Greene*

~Ready-to-Roll Emergency Containers ~

___1 change of clothes for each family member
___small hatchet, shovel and bucket
___cash in small bills
___$5 in coins for pay-phone calls
___pocket-size Holy Bible
___photocopies of personal documents (like wills, insurance, etc.)
___1 gallon of water per family member
___fruit leathers, granola bars, chewing gum
___battery-powered radio
___1 quart cooking pan
___flashlight, batteries
___small camping cookstove
___backpack for each family member
___first-aid kit
___sleeping bags
___insect repellant
___mouthwash
___toothbrushes & toothpaste
___coloring books & crayons
___pencils & notepad
___card games (i.e., Uno, Rook, etc.)
___1 can of tuna per family member
___2 instant soup packets per family member
___2 instant hot cocoa packets per family member
___feminine needs
___candles & matches
___can opener
___disposable drinking cups, utensils, plates
___water purifying tablets
___garbage bags
___infant needs (i.e., wet wipes, diapers, fever/pain reliever)
   ✍ Check your containers every 3-6 months
      and replace or add items as needed. ✍

Home Canning

" Plan your preserving, ladies, and try to have your fruit ready early in the morning before the heat of the day. Do not undertake to do too much at a time. Have your jars washed and sterilized, your preserving kettle cleaned and ready. Your tested recipe should be at hand so you do not have to waste time hunting for it. With these matters attended to, you may proceed with your mind clear of minor worries. When your canning is completed and the jars cooled and ready for storing, wash your face, brush your hair, brew yourself a nice cup of tea and set down and rest a spell." ~ *Advice from an Old Cookbook* ~

Excerpted from <u>Sleeping with a Sunflower</u>, p.140 by Louise Riotte © 1987
Used with permission from Storey Publishing, LLC

General Supplies Needed for Canning
pressure cooker (7 jar capacity)
large canner pot (7 jar capacity)
canning lids with rubber seal and rings
glass pint or quart-size canning jars
wide-mouth canning funnel
large slotted spoon
jar lifter
tongs

There is a wonderful, satisfying feeling that comes from a hard day's work of canning the produce from your garden bounty. When the day is done, you can sit back and admire the rows of jars filled with beans, apple pie filling or whatever you have preserved. In the olden days, your great-granny might not have had the proper equipment to ensure home-canned goods were always safe to eat. Today, if you follow directions and use the proper equipment, it is perfectly safe. You can control what goes into your jars. You can control the sugar and sodium content and never is there a need to add any chemical preservatives!

Home canning is achieved by either of these methods:

WATER BATH PROCESS

STEAM PRESSURE CANNER PROCESS

Water Bath Process

Use this process for foods that are high in acid content or have had vinegar added. It is sometimes referred to as the open kettle method. Before pressure cookers, this is the way all food was canned but it is not safe for vegetables, meats or other low-acid foods. It is safe and the recommended method to can with a water bath process the following foods:

Tomatoes
Pickles & Chow-Chows
Fruits & Pie Fillings
Sauerkraut

For this process, you will need a large pot with a tight-fitting lid and a rack that will fit in the pot to keep jars from sitting directly on the bottom of the pot.   It must be a large enough pot so that the quart or pint-size jars you are using will be completely covered by one inch of water while they are processing. About 11 inches or taller is a sufficient size if you are processing quarts. A jar-lifter tong would be handy to have to lift the hot jars from the water. Canning jars and lids with rubber seals and screw bands to fit your jars will be needed to hold your food stuffs.

Steps to the Process:

1 ~ Put the filled jars, with lids and bands screwed on tightly, into the pot that is half-full of boiling water. Pour in more boiling water if needed to cover the jars with one inch of water.

2 ~ When water is at a rolling boil, begin the timing.

3 ~ When the recommended processing time has elapsed, remove hot jars carefully from the pot with a jar-lifter tong and place on a towel covered surface.

4 ~ Leave undisturbed overnight. Check for a good seal (lid should not "pop" easily when pressed and the lid will be indented slightly). Remove the screw band and wipe jars clean. Label and store in your pantry.

Steam Pressure Canner Process

This is the only safe method for preserving meats, vegetables and other low-acid foods. You do not need to be afraid of the pressure canner. Follow all the directions and keep your canner in good working order and it will serve you well. Follow your canning cookbook or pressure canner manual for correct timing of the food you are processing.

1 ~ Place filled jars, with lids and bands screwed on tightly, down into the canner (with rack on bottom) with the recommended amount of hot water in the canner. Place jars evenly around in canner for good circulation.
2 ~ Put on high heat and lock the lid in place. Allow steam to escape from the vent for a few minutes before placing on the weight control so the cooker will begin to build up steam. When the cooker shows the correct amount of pressure on the gauge, reduce heat slightly. The weight will jiggle while processing to keep the pressure weight steady. Begin the timing process as soon as the pressure required is reached.
3 ~ When time has elapsed, removed the canner from the heat source. Allow the pressure to return to zero on it's own. Do not open the control valve or immerse in cold water! When pressure has dissipated, unlock the lid and remove hot jars with a jar-lifter tong. Place jars on a towel-covered surface. Let sit undisturbed overnight.
4 ~ Check seals and remove screw bands. Rinse off jars and dry. Label and store in the pantry for up to 1 year.
NOTE: Your pressure canner will come with a complete guide and instruction booklet for your type of canner and you need to follow those instructions as they are for your canner type.
TIP ~ No need to pay high prices for brand new canning jars. Jars can be found regularly at thrift stores, yard sales, and estate sales.

Resources for Home Canning

<u>Mrs. Wages NEW Home Canning Guide</u>
PO Box 2067, Tupelo, MS 38803-2067
by Precision Foods, Inc.

<u>The Ball Blue Book</u>
"The Guide to Home Canning and Freezing"
The Alltrista Corporation
PO Box 2729
Muncie, IN 47307

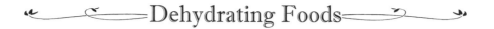

Dehydrating Foods

Most foods can be easily and successfully dried with very little preparation time. What's more, they are even easier to use!

~ Mrs. Marilyn Moll

Advantages of Dried Foods

Easily Stored ~ Dried foods take one-tenth or less the storage space of canned foods.

Naturally Good and Nutritious ~ Flavor and nutrition are kept in dried foods without adding preservatives, sugar, or salt. Dried fruits and some vegetables (such as seasoned zucchini chips) are great natural snacks.

Economical ~ Bottles, jars, lids, sugar, etc. are just some of the items you won't have to buy when you dry food. Processing energy will also be lowered considerably. Overripe fruit need not be thrown away but can be converted into tasty fruit leathers.

Completely Safe ~ Dried Foods (even vegetables and meats) are completely safe when dried according to directions. There is no danger of botulism because the moisture which is the breeding ground for organisms has been removed.

Versatile ~ Dried foods are easily reconstituted for use in many recipes, from main dishes to breads and deserts. Leftovers and peelings can be dried for flavoring soup stock.

Easily Prepared ~ For people in a hurry, drying is the ideal way to preserve food. Very little preparation is needed. No hot jars, canners, or boiling water to tend.

Food Preparation for Dehydrating

The smaller a piece of food, the faster it will dry. Ideally, slices or pieces should be a about ¼ inch thick.

Remove all pits from fruits before drying.

Before drying whole prunes, figs, and grapes they should be placed in boiling water or steam blanched for 1-2 minutes or pricked with a fork. This process allows moisture to escape during drying.

Vegetables should be blanched or steamed before being dried. This hastens the drying process, enhances the flavor, and preserves vitamin content.

Some fruits darken during the drying process. If you find these color changes objectionable, food pieces may be dipped in a solution of lemon juice, orange juice, pineapple juice, ascorbic acid, or sodium bisulfite prior to drying.

Food should be dried at its peak of freshness and ripeness. If foods cannot be dried immediately, they should be temporarily stored in a dark, cool location.

Used with permission
©Marilyn Moll of the Urban Homemaker

❧Resources❧
Preserving Foods at Home? Find supplies from:
The Urban Homemaker
Call for a Free Catalog
800.552.7323

Grow and Dry Your Own Seasonings

Basil

Easy to grow from seed ❧ Harvest in summer ❧ Dry leaves on stem ❧ After dry, strip leaves and crumble ❧ Use to season Italian dishes, vegetable soups, and pizza sauce.

Chives

Harvest through the growing season ❧ Clip leaves 3 inches from base ❧ Chop fine with kitchen scissors ❧ Dry to use in sour cream dips, soups, and salads.

Dill

Grows from seed easily ❧ Pick first blossom heads and throughout blooming season ❧ Flower heads can be left on stem to dry and then dill seeds strip easily, but you will lose some seeds that fall to the ground as the heads dry naturally ❧ Flower heads and leaves can be used in pickle making, or can be used in rye breads. Has a taste similar to caraway.

Mint

Harvest throughout the growing season ❧ Dry leaves on stems and strip off leaves when dry ❧ Spreads prolifically throughout the garden unless contained ❧ Leaves used most commonly in tea.

Parsley

Harvest throughout the growing season ❧ Dry leaves on stems and strip when dry ❧ Used in many recipes for color and mild flavor.

Rosemary

Best grown from a rooted cutting ❧ Has needle-like leaves ❧ Clip stems with leaves in 6 inch lengths before plant blooms (has cone-shaped deep lavender blossoms) ❧ Make small bundles, tied in center with a cotton string or raffia ❧ Use dried, crushed leaves for seasoning roasted poultry dishes.

Thyme

Harvest leaves all through growing season ❧ Dry and then strip tiny leaves from stems ❧ Use in seasoning poultry dishes, fish, vegetables, and casseroles.

154

Easy Bag Drying Method

Rinse the harvested stems of herbs and remove any dead or damaged leaves or stems. Gather small bundles together by the stems and tie them in bunches with some cotton string. Place the herb "bouquets" with the leaf side going in first into a small brown paper bag. Tie a cotton string firmly around the neck of the bag about 3 inches from the top. Cut 4 small slits in in the sides of the bag for air to circulate. Hang the bag in a warm, dry place for 10 days. Remove herbs from the bag. Strip leaves from stems and crumble between fingers. For extra-fine grind, whirl in a food processor equipped with a knife blade. Lay on a baking sheet in a thin layer and heat for 8 minutes in 200° oven. Let cool completely and store in a capped glass jar. Label. If herbs are not completely dry they will mold during storage. Well-dried herbs keep for up to 1 year, retaining a good flavor.

Freezing Foods

Most households have freezers as part of the household refrigerator for small items like ice cubes, ice cream and small amounts of meat or vegetables. If you are fortunate enough to have a larger freezer for preserving surplus foods, use it wisely.

Resources for Freezing How-To

<u>Stocking Up III</u>
"The All-New Edition of America's Classic Preserving Guide"
by
Carol Hupping and Staff of Rodale Food Center
ISBN: 0-87857 613-4

<u>Kerr Kitchen Cookbook</u>
"Home Canning and Freezing Guide"
PO Box 67961
Los Angeles, CA 90076

<u>The Ball Blue Book</u>
"The Guide to Home Canning and Freezing"
The Alltrista Corporation
PO Box 2729
Muncie, IN 47307

HELP! My freezer isn't working!

Call the electric company and let them know your power is off if that is the situation. If power is still working in other areas of your house, check the circuit breaker to the freezer power source. Check to make sure the plug has not been accidentally disconnected from the outlet. If all these things are in order, you will need to call a repairman. To reserve every bit of cold air possible, do NOT open your freezer. If the freezer will not be repaired for a period of more than 24 hours, purchase dry ice and place in freezer. Put in a layer of cardboard first to keep dry ice from coming in contact with foods. Open freezer ONLY to add in dry ice. This should keep your freezer cold enough to save your food goods until it can be repaired or replaced.

Freezer Log

~ Record goods put away in the freezer for a later day ~

Photocopy this page and keep on a clipboard with pencil
attached by a ribbon and hang on a peg near your freezer.

Date	Item	Date	Item
____	_____	____	_____
____	_____	____	_____
____	_____	____	_____
____	_____	____	_____
____	_____	____	_____
____	_____	____	_____
____	_____	____	_____
____	_____	____	_____
____	_____	____	_____
____	_____	____	_____
____	_____	____	_____
____	_____	____	_____
____	_____	____	_____
____	_____	____	_____
____	_____	____	_____
____	_____	____	_____
____	_____	____	_____
____	_____	____	_____
____	_____	____	_____
____	_____	____	_____
____	_____	____	_____
____	_____	____	_____

Household Freezer

Brand:_____

Purchased at:_____

Price:_____

Size:_____cu.ft.

Model No.:_____

Savory Chicken Vegetable Soup

Place in large pot and bring to a simmer:
24 cups chicken broth
3 cloves garlic, chopped
1 ½ teaspoons basil leaves
1 ½ teaspoons celery salt
¾ teaspoon ground ginger
3 tablespoons soy sauce
3 cups carrots, shredded or diced
3 cups potatoes, diced
3 cups cut green beans
3 cups green peas
3 cups corn kernels
3 large tomatoes, diced
6 cups chicken, cooked and chopped
2 small onions, diced
2 teaspoons salt or to taste
Ladle hot soup into clean, sterilized quart jars. Wipe rims clean and adjust lids and rings. Process for 90 minutes at 15 lbs. pressure in a pressure canner. Makes 14 quarts with a bit leftover to serve for your supper. May be frozen instead of canned, if desired.

Vernon's Venison

Prepare venison in 1 ½ inch chunks, free from sinew.
Place chunks in a large pot and add in:
water to nearly cover chunks
sprinkling of onion salt
sprinkling of garlic powder
1 beef bouillon cube for every 4 cups of venison chunks
Simmer meat chunks just until pink color is gone.
Stuff meat chunks into clean, sterilized, wide-mouth quart jars using a slotted spoon. Fill jars and pack in meat leaving a 1 inch headspace. Cover meat with reserved juices. Wipe rims clean and adjust lids and rings. Process in a pressure canner for 90 minutes at 15 lbs. pressure. Makes your venison tasty, juicy, and tender enough to flake with a fork!

Creamy Tomato Soup

Wash, core and do not peel:
14 quarts of tomatoes, sliced
Cook all together in a large pot on medium heat:
2 bay leaves
1 large bunch fresh parsley
7 chopped onions
1 tablespoon celery seed
14 quarts sliced tomatoes
Cook until simmering and simmer for 30 minutes, stirring
occasionally and being careful not to let it scorch.
Put thru a food sieve to strain out large pieces of
spice and tomato skin.
In a separate bowl, stir together:
1 cup flour
1 cup sugar
1 teaspoon baking soda
6 teaspoons salt
Mix well and stir in a few cups of hot tomato mixture and whisk to get
out any lumps. Add in to rest of tomato mixture in large pot and stir
well. Simmer for 20 minutes. Ladle into hot, clean quart or pint jars.
Wipe rims clean and adjust lids and bands on jars. Process in a water
bath for 20 minutes to preserve and seal jars.
To serve: Heat through and then add in ½ jar of milk. Heat just until
warm and do not boil. Delicious with grilled cheese sandwiches!

Zesty Dill Pickles

Use small-medium cucumbers. Rinse, scrub, rinse. Cut into 1-inch thick
slices or pickle whole or in spears. Fill jars with clean cucumbers.
Into each filled quart jar, put:
1 teaspoon dill seed or 1 head fresh dill
5 peppercorns
1/8 teaspoon red pepper flakes
1 small pinch of alum powder
2 whole garlic cloves
1/8 teaspoon turmeric
1 tablespoon onion flakes
Pour boiling brine over all. Process in water bath for 5 minutes.

BRINE: 13 cups water + 6 cups vinegar + ½ cup pickling salt

Cowboy Beans

Soak 8 pounds of small, white, dried
beans (Great Northern or Navy) overnight.
Pour off water and cover with fresh water and simmer for 1 hour.
Simmer in another large pot:

5 pounds of ham, cut into small chunks

2 tablespoons salt

4 quarts tomato juice

1 large onion, chopped fine

3 cups water

3 cups sugar

4 cups brown sugar

2 bottles ketchup (26 ounces each)

½ teaspoon cayenne pepper

1 teaspoon dry mustard

½ teaspoon cinnamon

Pour off cooking water and ladle hot beans into clean quart jars, filling
only two-thirds full. Fill remainder of jars with tomato liquid. Wipe
rims clean and adjust lids and bands. Process in a pressure canner for 90
minutes. Makes 15 quarts.

Oven Apple Butter

Peel apples, core, and cut into medium-size pieces. Place in a large pot
with one inch of water in the bottom. Cook apples until soft. Mash.
Measure out 2 quarts into an oven-proof crock or baking dish.

Add in:

2 ½ cups sugar

½ cup brown sugar

½ tablespoon cinnamon

1 teaspoon nutmeg

Cook for 3 - 4 hours at 350 degrees until thick and dark. Test for
doneness by dropping a spoonful of apple butter on a saucer. Should be
thickened and not surrounded by any liquid. Ladle into clean pint jars
and wipe rims clean. Adjust lids and bands. Process in a water bath for
15 minutes to seal. Remove jars from water. Let cool and remain
undisturbed for 24 hours. Rinse and dry jars to remove any residue.
Label.

Meatballs for the Freezer

2 pounds ground meat (turkey, venison, beef or pork)
1 sleeve saltine crackers, crushed (about 4 ounces)
¾ cup beef broth (use hot water + 1 bouillon cube)
4 eggs
¼ cup onion, chopped
2 teaspoons salt
½ teaspoon garlic powder
½ teaspoon black pepper

Mix all together. Scoop onto a baking sheet with a small size ice-cream scoop. This is a fast way to form the meatballs! Bake at 350° for 15-20 minutes. Check for doneness. Cool and freeze in freezer bags in portion sizes. Multiply recipe to make extra large batches for the freezer. Use in stroganoff, spaghetti sauce or mushroom gravy for a quick meal.

Apple Pie Filling

Peel, core, and slice 6 pounds of tart apples. Keep prepared apples immersed in water containing a tablespoon of lemon juice, to prevent browning while preparing filling syrup.
In a large saucepan blend together:
4½ cups sugar
1 cup cornstarch
2 teaspoons ground cinnamon
¼ teaspoon ground nutmeg
1 teaspoon salt
Add in and cook and stir until thickened:
10 cups water
3 tablespoons lemon juice

Pack apples into clean, sterilized quart jars up to 1 inch of the neck of jar. Fill with hot, thick syrup. Do not fill to top but leave a bit of headspace. Use a spatula to help distribute syrup. Wipe rims clean and adjust lids and bands. Process in a boiling water bath for 20 minutes.
Makes 6 quarts.

To serve: Prepare a double crust pastry. Line pie plate with pastry and add in 1 quart of pie filling. Dot with butter. Top with 2nd pastry crust, crimp and seal edges. Cut slits for steam to escape. Brush with milk and sprinkle with sugar. Bake on a baking sheet, lined with foil, to catch drips. Bake at 400° for 45-50 minutes. Serve warm with a dollop of whipped cream, vanilla ice cream, or a slab of Cheddar cheese.

161

Bread 'n Butter Pickles

Wash and thinly slice 4 quarts of cucumbers with peel on.
In a large tub, layer sliced cucumbers with 6 medium onions, thinly
sliced, 6 tablespoons of pickling salt, and crushed ice.
Let stand for 3 hours. Drain well.
In a large pot boil together:
3 cups cider vinegar
5 cups sugar
1 ½ teaspoons turmeric
1 ½ teaspoons celery seed
2 tablespoons mustard seed
Add in drained cucumbers and onions. Bring mixture back to a boil.
Remove from heat and pack with juice into clean pint jars. Wipe rims
and adjust lids and rings. Process in a water bath for 5 minutes.

Blackberry Jam

Rinse 5 cups of freshly picked blackberries.
Crush and measure out into a bowl, exactly 5 cups.
In a separate bowl, measure out exactly 7 cups sugar.
Place 5 cups crushed blackberries in a large saucepan
and add in 1 box of powdered pectin. Bring to a boil, while stirring constantly. All at once, add in the 7 cups of sugar. Stir constantly until mixture comes back to a full rolling boil. Boil and stir on medium high heat
for 1 full minute. Remove from heat and ladle into clean pint jars. Wipe
rims clean and adjust lids and screw-on bands. Process in a water bath
for 10 minutes. Makes 9 cups.

Homestyle B~B~Q Sauce

Simmer together in a large pot:
16 cups ketchup
4 cups brown sugar
½ cup liquid smoke
½ cup Worcestershire™ sauce
3 tablespoons garlic powder
2 tablespoons black pepper
¼ cup soy sauce
Ladle into clean pint jars. Wipe rims and adjust lids and bands.
Process in a boiling water bath for 20 minutes.

Reserve Records

Record here the home canned foods, dried foods
or emergency reserves you have stocked.

Favorite Preservin' Recipes

_____

_____
_____
_____
_____
_____
_____
_____
_____
_____
_____
_____
_____
_____
_____

_____
_____
_____
_____
_____
_____
_____
_____
_____
_____
_____
_____
_____
_____

Use this blank page for journaling or attach snippets and clippings for keepsakes.

Handiwork

Use this blank page for journaling or attach snippets and clippings for keepsakes.

*What is stitched in love is
hard to tear apart.*

Use this blank page for journaling or attach snippets and clippings for keepsakes.

The Sewing Basket

"I want a tidy life, neat as a woman's workbasket. Tasks wound on separate spools that unravel in single-thread, logical fashion. Ideas that keep filling the basket; good cloth to make things. Dreams that lie close, though separate as a woman's collection of buttons. A mind that is stern as the scissor that cuts the cloth to shape. Pains sharp and keen as needles to sew all the pieces together, and Love. . .like the basket itself, firm-woven, strong and cradling."

Attributed to Pauline Henderson

Items for the Sewing Basket

Spools of thread
minimum of one spool each: white, black and blue
Scissors
1 pair of shears for larger projects
1 small pair for trimming and handiwork
Seam ripper
Tape measure
Assortment of needles
Pincushion
Embroidery hoop
Assortments of embroidery floss
Beeswax ball
strengthens threads and helps prevent tangling
Thimble
leather, cloth, or metal varieties are available
Assorted sizes of safety pins
Needle threader
Assorted snaps, hooks & eyes
Iron-on patches
Sewing gauge
Small tin or jar of assorted buttons
Small crochet hook & sweater repair hook
Small bottle of fabric glue
for quick repairs

Contributed by ~ *Mrs. Rebekah Wilson*
Hope Chest Legacy ~ PO Box 1398 ~ Littlerock, CA 93543
888.554.7292

Basic Sewing Skills

The basic skills needed to sew for a family and home fall into two categories. The first is handsewing skills and the second is machine-sewing skills. Both work together to complement each other and are skills that a keeper of her home will find necessary. Although machine sewing is much quicker and easier than handsewing, there are handsewing skills every woman should know by the time she sets up her own home. Once learned, these essential skills allow for personalized taste, frugality and conservative dress. A homekeeper can make simple garments, curtains, household items and gifts at a fraction of the cost of purchased garments and goods. If the household monies are sparse, these skills will not go unpracticed.

Remember the old proverb -
"The wife's providence is to save. . .her husband's is to earn."

~ Essential Handsewing Skills ~

____ threading a needle and knotting the thread

____ sewing on a button

____ sewing a hem

____ basic mending stitch

____ 4 basic hand stitching and embroidery stitches

~ Essential Machine-Sewing Skills ~

____ learn to thread and operate your machine

____ sew in a straight line

____ sew a machine-stitched hem

____ sew a casing for elastic

____ make gathers and pleats

____ make a buttonhole

____ sew in a zipper

____ assemble and sew pieces from a cut pattern

Tip for Beginners

New machine sewers can sew on plain paper for practice. Trace a simple design like straight lines or a box on paper. Sew over the paper with your machine unthreaded. This lets you practice sewing in a straight line and turning corners with your machine. Once you are able to sew straight lines, trace curved and wavy lines and then circles and practice on those. To practice hemming, simply fold over the edge of paper and practice making a hem. Practicing this way is easy and allows you to have a basic idea of what to do when you start working with fabric, which can be a little harder to work with than stiff paper.

Tatters, tears, raveling threads and holes in our everyday garments are unavoidable. Every prudent homekeeper should be able to do simple mending repairs. Mending is a task that can be quickly started and finished if a well-equipped sewing basket is at hand. Keep it handy and you will not waste time searching for the items you need to sew on a loose button. The secret to mending is to not put it off! A few moment's attention to small repairs will reward you instantly by a garment or household item that is now able to be used right away, instead of being placed in the "mending basket" to be repaired later. Do not let your pile of mending stack up. It will become a discouraging sight to tired eyes to have that monumental task looming in your to-do list. Many a home has a "mending pile" filled to overflowing with garments that never find a needle and thread touching them, and at some future point they will be scooped up and thrown away. Keep your mending basket empty by repairing items regularly. With just a few moments of your time, each and every one of those items can be restored to full use and serve the purpose they were purchased for.

Buttons will pop off and need to be sewn back on. Keep a button jar of assorted colors and sizes handy for the one that falls off and cannot be found. Sewing a button on can be a simple little task that can be learned in a girl's early years.

A Basic Stitch

Hemming Stitch: This is a common handsewing stitch, used to sew layers of fabric together at the hem. The fabric is usually folded over and then folded over again. Where the edge of the folded fabric meets the flat fabric, the hem is placed with slightly slanted hemming stitches. The stitches should be placed about ¼ inch apart. Care should be taken to use small catch stitches on the side that will show. The threads should not be pulled tightly or you will have a puckered hem. This is a quick stitch once mastered with a little practice. See the illustration below.

Fold over ½ inch and over again for your hem allowance. The raw edge should always be neatly finished by turning under or encasing it with an over-lock stitch or hem tape. Pressing the hem in place helps make it easier to keep in place while stitching. You may need the assistance of pins or a long basting stitch to hold the hem in place until your hemming stitch is in place.

Embroidery

~ Threads ~

Use thread to co-ordinate with your work. Use lighter weight threads for light work on thin fabrics and heavier cotton threads for a rich, heavy look on weightier fabrics.

~ Needles ~

The needle with which you embroider opens the weave of the material to enable the threads to slide through easily. The eye should be slightly larger than the thickness of the embroidery thread. Embroidery needles have a longer eye than sewing needles.

~ Scissors ~

Embroidery scissors should be about 4 inches long and have very sharp points.

~ Beginnings & Finishings ~

The wrong side of your work should look equally as good as the right side. To begin a piece of embroidery do not use a knot, but make a close running stitch toward the starting point. Then make a small back stitch and begin to embroider in the direction specified. To end your thread, weave the needle in and out of the material under the piece which has just been completed, but do not allow your needle to pick up any of the embroidery stitches. When you feel the end of the thread is secure, cut the thread close. Do not carry the thread from one design to the other as this produces very untidy work.

~ Pressing ~

All embroidery should be pressed on a thickly padded surface. The raised face of the embroidery sinks into the softness of the padding and it is not flattened by the iron. Always place your work wrong side up. Cover with a damp cloth. Press with a moderately hot iron. Remove the damp cloth and iron dry, being careful not to scorch.

~ Frames or Hoops ~

Frames are adjusted over a small area of work and the material is held taut and cannot pucker. They are available in several shapes and sizes.

Adapted from ~ "LEARN HOW BOOK" ~ No.170
©1941 The Spool Cotton Company with permission from Coats&Clark, Inc.

Simple Embroidery Stitches

CHAIN STITCH: Holding work toward you, bring the thread up through the line you have traced and hold it down with the left thumb. Pass needle through the same place again and bring it out about one-eighth inch in front of previous stitch.

SATIN STITCH: Straight stitches worked closely together.

LAZY DAISY: Worked exactly like chain stitch except that each stitch is held in position with a small stitch at center of loop.

SEED STITCH: Small straight stitches worked in every direction.

BUNDLES: Make groups of 3 or 4 straight stitches. Then make one or two vertical stitches at center.

COUCHING: Lay a thread across couching line, then with a contrasting color sew the laid thread in place with small stitches at equal distances apart.

BLANKET STITCH: Bring needle up on right side, hold thread under left thumb, insert needle about one-fourth inch to the right and bring it out through loop held by left thumb.

BACK STITCH: Bring needle out on right side, insert it back one-eighth inch behind first stitch and bring it out one-eighth inch in front of first stitch.

FRENCH KNOT: Draw point of needle through fabric to right side; wind thread around needle three times. Insert needle in fabric very close to where the needle came up and pull through to wrong side, holding twists in place with thumb of left hand.

Stitches & Illustrations from "LEARN HOW BOOK" ~ No. 170
©1941 The Spool Cotton Company used with permission Coats&Clark, Inc.

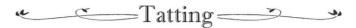

Tatting

Tatting differs entirely from crochet, and is composed of stitches forming knots. To make the stitches or knots a small instrument is used, called a shuttle. This shuttle consists of two oval pieces, flat on one side and convex on the other, and is made of wood or ivory.
Beeton's Book of Needlework
by ~ Mrs. Isabella Mary Beeton ~
published by Ward, Lock and Tyler, 1870

Supplies: tatting shuttle and cotton thread in size 20 or 30. First you will fill your shuttle with the cotton thread and do not wind past the edge of the shuttle and <u>do not</u> cut thread from the ball.

Make the ring:
   Wrap the center of the uncut thread around the finger tips of the left hand and cross the threads between the forefinger and thumb without knotting. This forms the ring. Hold the shuttle in the right hand with the pointed end facing the left hand and the thread coming from the back of the shuttle.

First half of double stitch:
   Make a loop with the shuttle thread on top of the left hand, clockwise from left to right. Pass the shuttle through the center of the left hand and upwards through the loop. The shuttle thread forms a stitch around the ring thread. This stitch is the first half of the double stitch and <u>must</u> be <u>transferred</u> to the ring thread: <u>Relax</u> the fingers of the left hand and pull the shuttle thread <u>taut</u>. This action will transfer the first half stitch to the ring thread (the ring thread forms the knot around the straight shuttle thread).

   Raise the middle finger of the left hand and pull the shuttle to the right, keeping the shuttle thread <u>taut</u>. This is important to prevent the shuttle thread from forming the knot around the ring thread. Keeping the shuttle thread taut also allows the stitch to slide along it to the left hand thumb. The stitch will slide towards the left hand thumb. Hold the stitch firmly between the left hand thumb and forefinger.

178

Second half of the double stitch:

Make the second half of the stitch by passing the shuttle through the space between the middle and the ring finger of the left hand. Take the shuttle through the ring and to the right. Transfer the second half of the stitch from the shuttle thread to the ring thread by relaxing the thread on the left hand and pulling the shuttle thread taut. These two half stitches form one double stitch (in patterns often referred to as "ds".)

Testing:

Pull the bottom thread of the ring around the left hand. If it enlarges the ring itself, the stitches have transferred correctly. If it does not move, the stitches have locked (the shuttle thread formed the knot around the ring thread) and must be picked loose and undone. Try again. The stitches must move freely on the ring thread.

As you progress:

To enlarge the ring around the left hand, pull the bottom thread of the ring. Do the test and the enlarging of the ring every few stitches to ensure that all the stitches have all transferred correctly and the ring can be pulled closed later.

PULL THE RING THREAD ANTI-CLOCKWISE TO MAKE THE RING LARGER

Picots:

Picots are made by leaving a space <u>between</u> two double stitches. They are made to decorate the work and also serve as a joining point.

PICOT STARTING TO FORM

PICOT

To close a ring:

After making the required amount of double stitches and picots, close the ring by pulling the shuttle thread and carefully holding the last stitches, until the ring is completely closed. Where spaces left between the double stitches to form picots, the ring thread will now form small loops—the picots.

Instructions and illustrations used with permission
~ Marie Potgieter ~ Experienced Tatter ~
Rootepoort, South Africa

179

Tatting can become very detailed and the patterns intricate. The previous instructions are just to get started. Many good books filled with patterns and illustrations are available. More advanced stitches using a shuttle and separate ball of thread are used to make chains and to do reverse work. New threads of various colors can be joined with other methods to make your project have a varied color scheme. It is a lovely old-fashioned skill that gives hours of enjoyment to the lady and produces beautiful edgings for doilies, handkerchiefs, napkins, and tea towels. It can be carried in a small bag to keep hands busy when they otherwise might have to sit idle.

Resources

HANDY HANDS TATTING
557 N. 1800 E.
Paxton, Illinois 60957 USA
217.379.3976 ~ Mail Order Only
Newsletter subscriptions available filled with tatting patterns and projects.
Pewter shuttles, supplies, threads.

THREADS
522 S. 48 Street
Lincoln, NE 68516
800.248.8959

Simple Tatted Edging
Use on guest towels, hankies, and for trimming heirloom baby garments.

R (ring) of 4 ds (double stitches), 3 p's (picots) sep. (separated) by 5 ds, 4 ds, cl (close); * sp (space) of ¼ inch; r (ring) of 4 ds, join to the last p of previous r, 5 ds, 2 p's sep. by 5 ds, cl. Repeat from * for length desired.

TIP: When a new thread is required make a square knot close to the base of the last ring or chain, but do not cut off the ends, for the strain of the work may loosen the knot. If you make a knot in the thread, cut if off and tie the new thread close to the last ring. Knots prevent the ring from being drawn up, for they will not pass through the double stitches. Cut off loose ends later.

My Stitching Projects

Write pattern numbers, attach swatches of fabrics, or write descriptions and / or paste photographs of projects you have stitched.

My Stitching Projects

My Stitching Projects

Quilting

Heirloom Quilts to Treasure

"Colonial winters were cold, and the log houses of the colonists drafty. But the busy English and Dutch housewife kept her scraps and pieced them together, and the members of her household did not suffer. Large, warm quilts covered the beds, heavy quilted curtains were drawn over the windows, and quilted petticoats were part of every woman's wardrobe.

The patchwork quilts were the ones of which the quiltmaker was proudest, while the piecework bed coverings were most common. This is not so difficult to understand when you remember that the materials had to be either laboriously woven in the home or imported. The appliqué (or patched) quilt, calling for a large, un-pieced background and large pieces was a luxury and a showpiece. But the pieced quilts, using every available scrap of new and old material, were constantly being made and were on every bed. The Crazy Quilt is the oldest and one of the most common of colonial pioneer days because it made use of even the tiniest and most irregularly-shaped scraps.

When the quilt was "ready for the frame" it was the custom to ask the women of the neighborhood to come and help with the quilting. Thus, the quilt making was not only a household art born of family needs, but an interest drawing the busy women into social groups.

The patterns used, many of which have come down to us, were often inspirations of the home: Cake Stand, Windmill, Dresden Plate, and the Tea Leaf. The Bible, so large a factor in daily life, was responsible for such names as Rob Peter to Pay Paul and Jacob's Ladder. The New World worked itself into the quilts in Bear's Paw, Crossed Canoes, Turkey Track, Log Cabin and Arrowhead. These and thousands of others have spread with the population and now may be found in every part of the country.

While only a few of the many truly beautiful old quilts have been preserved, quilt making itself has passed from mother to daughter, and today, many homes and community groups are producing worthy descendants of this splendid art.

The padding for quilts comes in sheets of cotton manufactured especially for quilts. Quilting was invented to hold the padding in place. Elaborate patterns came as an afterthought.

For most designs, it is best to follow the outlines of the design. When the quilt is used on the lining side it will duplicate the pattern.

Special needles, short and slender, (but with large eyes), are manufactured for quilting, the most popular sizes running from 5 to 9. A variety of quilting transfers are sold by firms that handle needlework patterns and designs.

The quilting, done with No. 40 or 50 thread, should be started at one end and finished at the other, with the fullness kept ahead of the work. Some of the best quilt makers suggest the use of waxed thread for quilting.

A true bias binding, not more than one-half inch wide when finished, should be used for the edge of the quilt. If the corners of the quilt are slightly rounded a more perfect binding is possible.

Recently, I was told a lovely story of how an elderly woman enjoyed fingering over the various patches in a "crazy quilt" she had inherited. In one corner was a patch from her great-grandmother's very best "Sunday-go-to-meetin" silk dress. Over toward the middle was another in deep rose velvet from a cape her sister had worn the evening she had been "presented to society."

One day when she was not feeling well, she discovered best of all a verse which had been sketched into a patch with letters so tiny she had to use a magnifying glass to read them:

"Sleep Sweet within this quiet room, O thou, whoe'er thou art,
And let no mournful yesterdays disturb thy peaceful heart.
Nor let tomorrow mar thy rest with dreams of coming ill:
Thy maker is thy changeless friend, His love surrounds thee still.
Forget thyself and all the world, put out each garish light:
The stars are shining overhead ~ Sleep sweet! Good night!

~ Good night!"

Though she had used the quilt on her bed for many years, she had never noticed this verse before and she thought how strange it was that the words had been called to her attention at a time when she was depressed and needed them most. Then the thought came to her that every generation, with all its changes, has a "changeless Friend." Then she remembered something else— that "The Comforter" (which a quilt is often called) is another name for the "Holy Spirit."

With this story in mind I would suggest that when your quilt is finished, you embroider your signature and the date in one corner, identifying for all time the thing of beauty on which you have spent so many pleasurable hours. Your children and your children's children may be "comforted" by it.

from Sleeping with a Sunflower by Louise Riotte Copyright ©1987
Used with permission from Storey Publishing LLC

185

Simple Quilt Block Pattern

contributed by ~ *Mrs. Rebekah Wilson*

Items Needed:

Assorted fabrics - 100% cotton muslin, calico, or broadcloth. You will need both light and dark fabric for your quilt blocks.

Directions:

Using your ruler, measure out a square 4.5" x 4.5" on your paper or card-stock and cut your pattern on the lines. Place your pattern over your washed, dried, and ironed fabric. Pin in place. Cut around the pattern to make your first quilting piece. You will need two dark blocks and two light blocks. Make sure you cut two of each for every quilt block you plan to make.

With your first four quilt pieces, lay them on a tabletop. Place one dark piece down, and a light piece next to it. Beneath your dark piece put a light piece. A dark piece will fill in the missing corner. You have your pieces placed now.

Use your dark piece and lay the right side down onto the right side of the light piece next to it. Match up the edges and pin one side. Using a running stitch, sew a ¼-inch seam along the edge you have pinned, taking stitches as small and close together as you can make them. If you are using a sewing machine, sew along the edge.

When you are finished, repeat this with the last two pieces of fabric for your block. When both sets have been sewn, remove the pins and iron the seam flat - iron with the dark side of the seam on the dark side of the fabric so your seam fabric will not show through on the light colored side. Lay your pieces out as before. Now place the top piece onto the bottom piece and match up the seam. Pin with the dark side of the seam touching the dark side of the fabric. Pin the remaining edge and sew across. Remove pins and iron seam flat. You now have your first block.

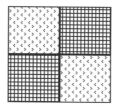

Four Patch
Design

Suggestions and Options:

Depending on what project you are making, you can continue to make more until all your blocks are complete or stop with this block. You will have a ¼" seam allowance left on all four corners of your block.

You may also create a nine piece quilt block by cutting five dark pieces and four light ones. A twenty-five piece quilt block is very nice and also dates back to the Colonial Days of America (there are many historic quilts made in this style on display in many Colonial museums). To make the twenty-five piece block, simply make your quilt block by using two dark pieces across the top row with three light pieces alternating. The next row would have two light pieces with three dark pieces alternating. Continue in this manner until you have five rows total. Be careful to match up ALL seams in each row and pin well prior to sewing. You might also want to make the square pieces smaller. A 2.5" x 2.5" is a good size or even a 3.5" x 3.5". This is a very good way to use up scraps and have a beautiful quilt for the effort.

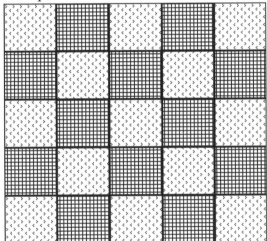

 Twenty-Five Patch
Design

" *She wrought herself a robe of grace as mother, friend and wife. . .from odds and ends of busy days, and tangled scraps of life.*"

~ by Frances McKinnon Morton

Crocheting

Illustrations and instructions excerpted from "LEARN HOW BOOK" ~ No. 170
©1941 The Spool Cotton Company used with permission Coats&Clark, Inc.

Practice a few of the first steps of crochet with heavy yarn and a No. 7 crochet hook, because the beginner can handle them easily, and almost before you know it, you will be ready to try out your newly acquired skill.

PRACTICE PIECES

Directions are given for a small practice piece or swatch consisting of a foundation chain of 20 stitches and 4 rows of the stitch which you are learning. This swatch can be quickly completed and the stitch can be easily applied in making attractive articles.

BEGIN BY MAKING A LOOP

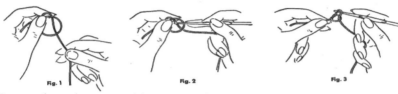

1. Grasp thread near end between thumb and forefinger of left hand.
2. Make loop by lapping long thread over short thread.
3. Hold loop in place between thumb and forefinger (Fig.1).
4. Take hold of broad bar of hook as you would a pencil.
5. Put your hook through loop, catch long end of thread, draw it through (Fig.2).
6. Do not remove hook from thread.
7. Pull short end and ball thread in opposite directions to bring loop close around the end of the hook but not too tight (Fig.3).

WHAT TO DO WITH THE LEFT HAND

1. Measure with your eye about 4 inches down ball thread from loop on needle.
2. At about this point, insert thread between your ring and little fingers. (Palm of hand facing up Fig.4)
3. Bring thread toward back, under little and ring fingers, over the middle finger, and under the forefinger toward the thumb (Fig.5).

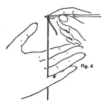 

4. Grasp needle and loop between thumb and forefinger of left hand.
5. Gently pull ball thread so that it lies around the fingers firmly but not tightly (Fig.6).
6. Catch knot of loop between thumb and forefinger.

Fig. 6

WHAT TO DO WITH THE RIGHT HAND

1. Take hold of broad bar of hook as you would a pencil.
2. Bring middle finger forward to rest near tip of hook (Fig. 7).

Fig. 7

BEFORE YOU BEGIN THE CHAIN STITCH

Adjust the fingers of left hand as in Fig.8. The middle finger is bent in such a way as to regulate the tension, while the ring and little fingers prevent the thread from moving too freely. As you practice you will become more familiar with the correct position. Keep in mind that the motion of the hook in the right hand and the thread in the left hand should be easy and smooth. One of the most common faults of beginners is either to crochet too tightly or too loosely. Ease will come with practice.

Fig. 8

CHAIN STITCH

1. Pass your hook under thread and catch thread with hook. (This is called "thread over" Fig.9).
2. Draw thread through loop on hook.
   This makes one chain (ch). Do not work tightly.
3. Repeat steps 1 and 2 until you have as many chains stitches as you need. One loop always remains on the hook (Fig.10).
4. Always keep thumb and forefinger of your left hand near stitch on which you are working.
5. Practice making chains until they are even in size.

Fig. 9

Fig. 10

SINGLE CROCHET

Make a foundation chain of 20 stitches for practice piece.

FIRST ROW

1. To begin row, insert hook from the front under the two top threads of second chain (ch) from hook (Fig.11).
2. Catch thread with hook ("thread over") (Fig.12) and draw through stitch (st). There are now two loops on hook (Fig.13).
3. Thread over and draw through two loops. (One loop remains on hook). One single crochet (s c) is now completed (Fig.14).
4. For next single crochet (s c), insert hook under two top threads of next stitch (st) and proceed as before. (Repeat steps 2 and 3).
5. Repeat until you have made a single crochet (s c) in every chain (ch).
6. At end of row of single crochets, chain (ch) 1 (Fig.15).
7. Turn your work so that the reverse side is facing you (Fig.16).

SECOND ROW

1. Insert the hook from the front under the two top threads of second stitch from hook. (First stitch on previous row).
2. Repeat steps 2,3,4,5,6, and 7 in directions for first row.

THIRD ROW

1. Repeat second row.

FOURTH ROW

1. At end of fourth row, do not make a turning chain.
2. Clip thread about 3 inches from work, bring loose end through the one loop remaining on hook and pull tightly (Fig.17).
3. Now you have completed your practice piece in single crochet.

NOTE: In all crochet it is customary to pick up the two top threads of every stitch as you work. If a different effect is desired, pick up only one top thread. This is known as the Rib Stitch.

TURNING YOUR WORK

In crochet a certain number of chain stitches is added at the end of every row to bring work in position for the next row. Then the work is turned so that the reverse side is facing the worker. You will notice that in single crochet, one chain only is used for turning. The number of turning chains depends upon the stitch with which you intend to begin the next row. The exact number will be indicated in the directions. The turning chain always counts as the first stitch.

DOUBLE CROCHET
Make a foundation chain of 20 stitches for practice piece.
FIRST ROW

Fig. 18

1. To begin row, thread over and insert hook from the front under the two top threads of 4th chain (ch) from hook (Fig.18).
2. Thread over and draw through stitch (st). There are now three loops on hook.

Fig. 19

3. Thread over (Fig.19) and draw through 2 loops. (Two loops remain on hook. Fig.20).

Fig. 20

4. Thread over again and draw through the two remaining loops. (One loop remains on hook). One double crochet (d c) is now completed. (Fig.21).
5. For next double crochet (d c) thread over, insert hook from the front under the two top threads of next stitch (st) and proceed as before. (Repeat steps 2, 3, and 4).
6. Repeat until you have made a double crochet (d c) in every chain.
7. At end of row, chain three (ch 3) (Fig.22) and turn. (The three chain stitches count as the first double crochet (d c) in next row).

Fig. 21

SECOND ROW

1. To begin row, thread over, insert the hook from the front under the two top threads of the fifth stitch from the hook. (Second stitch on previous row).

Fig. 22

Fig. 23

2. Repeat steps 2,3,4,5,6 and 7 (Fig.23).

191

THIRD & FOURTH ROWS

1. Repeat second row.
2. Finish off at end of fourth row by cutting the thread about 3 inches away from last double crochet (d c). Bring end through the loop and pull tightly.
3. Now you have completed your practice piece in double crochet.

SLIP STITCH

It is not necessary to make a practice piece for slip stitch (sl st) because it is used only in joining or when an invisible stitch is required. If the directions call for a slip stitch (sl st), refer to this page to see how it is done. When the directions say *join* you always use a slip stitch.

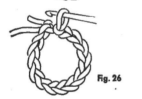

1. Insert hook from the front through the two top threads of stitch (st) (Fig.25).
2. Thread over and with one motion draw through stitch (st) and loop on hook. (1 loop remains on hook. Fig.26).

Fig. 25

Fig. 26

Practice these steps to begin crocheting. Then find a complete guide book with more details and further instructions on crocheting and try your hand at a project. Many crochet instruction booklets contain patterns for the beginner.

Resources

Leisure Arts Booklets from *Bows in Bloom*
PO Box 412 ~ Creola, AL 36525
Crocheting projects and many more detailed instructions
5009 = 32 page booklet ~ teaches 19 more crochet stitches
3104 = 40 page booklet ~ 10 great projects + lessons
75000 = 16 page booklet ~ dishcloths to knit and
crochet & small beginner projects

Knitting

Learning to knit is lots of fun.
You put on two, then take off one.
Missing a stitch and back you go.
And then you start another row.

Faster and faster, on I go.
I love to sit and watch it grow.
Only one thing that puzzles me,
When I get through, what will it be?

by ~ Verna Meade Surer

HOW TO WIND WOOL

When the wool is wound from a skein into a ball, great care should be taken not to stretch the yarn. One way of winding wool is to wrap a dozen or more strands around three fingers. Remove this bundle from the fingers. Lay in opposite direction, and wrap wool around fingers and over the bundle as well. Repeat this action until the whole skein is wound, being careful to always wind around the fingers. This will prevent any strain on the ball of yarn.

PRACTICE PIECES

All knitting is based on two stitches, the knit stitch and the purl stitch. To help you master these two stitches, directions are given for practice pieces of 20 stitches for 10 rows.

BEGINNING TO KNIT

For correct tension, as it is called, the stitches should fit closely but not tightly around the needles. They should move back and forth along the needles freely but not so loosely as to allow the needles to fall out. Relax while you work. Hold your needles and yarn easily. Avoid a cramped position. Lightness of touch gives speed and produces an even fabric. Use a set of knitting pins (needles) 4¼mm size (No.6) as they are easy for the beginner to handle.

CASTING ON....The First Step in Knitting
"Putting the first stitches on the needle is called casting on."

193

HOW TO BEGIN TO KNIT

1. To cast on 20 stitches you will need to measure off 16 inches of yarn, do not cut from ball (Fig.1).
2. Make a slip loop 16 inches from the end of the yarn (Fig.2-5).

Fig. 1

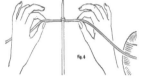

Fig. 2

Fig. 3

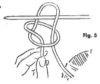

Fig. 4

3. Place the loop on the needle and gently pull the ends of the yarn (not too tight, Fig.6). The ball end of the yarn is to the right and the free end of the yarn is to the left.

Fig. 5

WHAT TO DO WITH THE RIGHT HAND

1. Place the needle between the thumb and first finger, as if you were holding a pencil (Fig.7).
2. Be sure that the loop is near the pointed end of the needle (Fig.7).
3. Using the ball end of the yarn, place the yarn loosely over the first finger, under the second, over the third, under the fourth above middle joint (Fig.7). The second and third fingers are very important because they keep the flow of yarn even, not too tight or not too loose, that is, they regulate the correct tension.

WHAT TO DO WITH THE LEFT HAND

1. Grasp the free end of the yarn lightly against the left hand with the second, third, and fourth fingers (Fig.8).
2. Place the yarn near the needle around and under the thumb (Fig.9).

Fig. 8

Fig. 9

3. Bring the hands close together and adjust the yarn. For position see Fig.10. and follow the steps on the next page to continue the procedure.

Fig. 10

PROCEDURE

1. Notice that the yarn makes a loop around the left thumb.
2. Insert your needle through the underside of the loop (Fig.10 & 11).
3. Bring the yarn in the right hand over the joint of the needle from the back (Fig.12).
4. Draw it through the loop (Fig.13).
5. Gently pull the free end of the yarn with the left hand to tighten the stitch (Fig.14).
6. Place the yarn around thumb as directed before and repeat steps 2–5 inclusive until you have 20 stitches.

Fig. 11

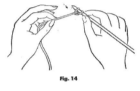

Fig. 12

Fig. 13

Fig. 14

THE KNIT STITCH
Plain Knitting or Garter Stitch

WHAT TO DO WITH THE LEFT HAND

1. In the left hand, hold the needle with the stitches just cast on. For position see Fig.15.
2. The first stitch is held lightly by the index finger near the tip of the needle (Fig.15).

WHAT TO DO WITH THE RIGHT HAND

1. Hold the needle between the thumb and the index finger, as if you were holding a pencil (Fig.16).
2. The yarn is placed over the first finger, under the second, over the third, and under the fourth above the middle joint. As you practice knitting, you will learn to adjust the yarn so that you will get the best results (Fig.16).

NOW YOU ARE READY

Bring your hands close together. Adjust the yarn and insert needle in first stitch as in Fig.17.

Fig. 15

Fig. 16

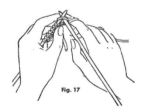

Fig. 17

195

KNIT STITCH PROCEDURE
~ First Row ~

1. Insert the right needle into the front of the first stitch on the left needle from the left side (Fig.18).
2. Steady the right needle against the forefinger of the left hand. Keep your yarn to the back of your work.
3. With the right hand bring the yarn over the point of the right needle (Fig.19).
4. Draw the yarn through the stitch (Fig.20).
5. Slip the old stitch off the left needle, thus completing the first stitch. A new row is being formed on the right needle (Fig.21).

6. Always keep pushing your work up so that the stitch on which you are working is near the tip of the needle.
7. Repeat steps 1-5 until all the stitches have been knitted off the left needle. An easy way to remember these steps is to repeat to yourself: *"In"* ~ (step 1-Fig.18) ~ *"Over"* ~ (step 2-Fig.19) ~ *"Through"* ~(step 3-Fig.20) ~ *"Off"* ~ (step 4-Fig.21).
8. Now you have knitted one row. You should have 20 stitches on the needle.

~ Second Row and Succeeding Rows ~

1. Change the needle with the stitches into the left hand.
2. The empty needle is in the right hand. The yarn is over the first fin ger under the second, over the third, and under the fourth above the middle joint (Fig.16).
3. Insert right needle into the front of the first stitch on the left needle from the right side and slip the first stitch off the left needle onto the right needle without knitting. Do this with the first stitch of each succeeding row and you will have a smooth edge known as a chain edge (Fig. 22).
4. Bring your yarn to the back of your work by passing it between the two needles.
5. Proceed as before (Fig.22).

Fig. 22

When you have worked 10 rows you are ready to finish off the swatch. This process is called binding off.

BINDING OFF PROCEDURE

1. Slip the first stitch on the row off the left needle onto the right needle without knitting.
2. Knit the second stitch very loosely. (There are two stitches on the right needle).
3. Insert the left needle through the left side of the first stitch (Fig.23).

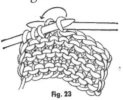

Fig. 23

4. Keep the yarn in the right hand very loose so that the second stitch remains loose.
5. Bring the first stitch forward over the second stitch and over the tip of the needle so that one stitch remains on the needle (Fig.23).
6. Knit the next stitch loosely. There are two stitches on the right needle.
7. Repeat steps 3 6 (Fig.23).
8. When you come to the last stitch, clip your yarn about three inches from the needle. Bring the loose end through the stitch remaining on the needle and pull tightly. Darn in loose end so that it will not show.

PURL STITCH
The purl stitch has two differences from the knit stitch.

1. In plain knitting you keep your yarn at the back of your work. In purling you bring it to the front of your work.
2. In plain knitting you insert your needle in the front stitch from the left side. In purling you insert your needle in the front of the stitch from the right side.

The purl stitch is not used alone, but when it is combined with the knit stitch in straight knitting, it makes another stitch known as the stockinette stitch.

If you have enjoyed trying your hand at these knitting stitches you will find further instruction in
"Knitter's Guide to Needles, Yarn and Stitching Techniques"
12 page Leaflet #56004, Leisure Arts Publications
Available from: Bows In Bloom, PO Box 412, Creola, AL 36525

Knitting illustrations & instructions excerpted from "LEARN HOW BOOK" ~ No. 170
©1941 The Spool Cotton Company used with permission Coats&Clark, Inc.

Seamstresses of yesteryear made their garments without patterns. Just some measuring and cutting, their hands flying nimbly with a needle, and they had a lovely garment. There are many patterns available on the market for you to use today. No guesswork is needed! Here are a few simple patterns with some hand-sketched illustrations. They are sure to become favorite stand-bys for you to make!

Momma's Favorite Apron

For an old-timey look, use gingham or calico.

Step #1

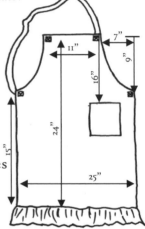

Cut out these pieces:

Straps ~ cut two (3 ½ inches x 36 inches)

Ruffle ~ cut one (6 inches x 45 inches)

Pockets ~ cut two (8 inches x 8 inches)

Main body ~ cut one by measurements on sketch

Step # 2

Zigzag or serge raw edges of top, curves, and sides of main body piece. Hem these edges by turning under 3/8 inch and stitching down with a straight stitch on the machine.

Step # 3

Prepare pockets by zigzagging the top edge. Then turn under 1 inch and stitch in place. Press under ½ inch on the remaining raw edges. Position on main body piece and stitch in place close to edges. Reinforce top corners of pocket by back-stitching.

Step #4

Prepare ruffle by zigzagging or serging sides and bottom edge. Turn up ½ inch and stitch the small hem in place. Run a gathering/basting thread across the top edge. Gather and adjust the gathers as necessary to fit the main body piece across the bottom edge. Stitch in place and then zigzag or serge raw edges of main body and ruffle edge together to make a neatly finished seam. Press.

Step #5

Prepare straps by folding in half with wrong sides together. Zigzag or serge together along raw edges. Press the straps flat, with stitched edges in center of strap. This is the under side and will not show when strap is sewn to main body. Sew one end of strap to right bib corner bringing across the back and sewing the other end to the left side near waist. Sew other strap to left bib corner and right side at waist edge. This attaches the straps in a criss-cross fashion and eliminates the need for tying your apron on.

Sketch of finished apron with appliqué on pocket and front. See below for an appliqué idea. Enlarge and trace onto apron and apply by appliqué or embroidery stitches.

Water Pot & Yo-Yo Flower
~ Embroidery or Applique Pattern ~

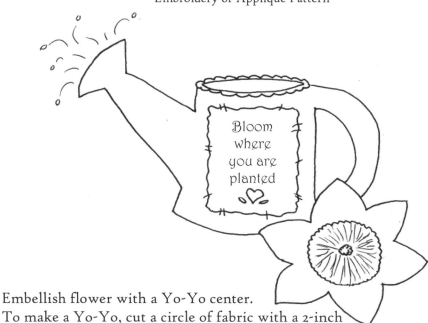

Bloom where you are planted

Embellish flower with a Yo-Yo center.
To make a Yo-Yo, cut a circle of fabric with a 2-inch diameter. Turn under a scant bit around the raw edge of the circle with your fingers while taking small running stitches with a needle and thread. When you have completed the running stitch all the way around the circle, pull thread up to gather up the circle. Finger press to flatten out circle and secure the thread thru the center "hole" a few times. Add to "flower" to make a perfect center. Tack on around the edges with hidden stitches, "flat" side towards the back.

An Apron for All Occasions

Years ago, the homekeeper had assorted aprons as part of her wardrobe. She wore them to cook, to clean, to garden and was rarely without her apron on, unless she was "going out." Victorian ladies spent hours embellishing their aprons with intricate details of tatted lace and embroidery on fine, white linen. Homekeepers of the Depression-era had to make do with whatever scraps they had available to fashion their aprons, even flour sacks were used. Sixty years ago, rarely was a homekeeper seen in a magazine advertisement without an apron on. They were the fashion; they were useful and they were a symbol of domestic pride. Embellished with all sorts of trims and buttons, most ladies had a wide assortment of styles for any occasion. We have such modern conveniences today and we can drop clothes in an automatic washing machine anytime. This has caused aprons to have lost their popularity. Aprons have not lost their usefulness, the homekeeper has just set them aside. Try stitching an apron from white, crisp cotton and embellishing it with pretty laces and ruffles. Wear it to serve your family a special dinner and you will feel as if you have stepped back in time. You will want to make more aprons in ginghams and denims for the tasks you must complete in your home. Don't forget to add the pockets, they certainly come in handy!

Inches O' Stitches Apron

Step # 1

Cut out these pieces:

Waistband ~ cut one (4 inches x 20 inches)
Tie sashes ~ cut two (2 inches x 44 inches)
Pockets ~ cut two (8 inches x 8 inches)
Apron skirt ~ cut one (38 inches x 22 inches)
You will need: 1 36-inch cloth measuring tape for embellishment

Step # 2

Zigzag or serge raw edge of both 22-inch sides of apron skirt. Hem these edges by turning under 1 inch and stitching in place with a straight stitch.

Prepare one 40-inch raw edge by serging or turning under ¾ inch and then again 2 inches. Press in place and stitch close to edge with a straight stitch.

Step # 3

Prepare pockets by zigzagging or serging the raw top edge. Then turn under 1 inch and stitch in place. Press under ½ inch on the remaining raw edges. Position on apron skirt and stitch in place close to edges, leaving top edge free. Reinforce top corners of pockets by back-stitching.

Step # 4

Finish tie sashes by folding over twice in a small ¼-inch rolled hem and stitching in place. Finish off 2 long edges and 1 short end.

Step # 5

Gather the top edge of apron skirt with a long basting stitch. Fold waistband in half lengthwise and press. Place waistband on gathered apron skirt, adjusting gathers to fit, leaving ½-inch of waistband protruding past apron skirt. (Ties will be stitched on here.) Match raw edges of waistband and raw top edge of apron skirt. Stitch waistband in place. Finish off seam with a zigzag stitch or by serging. Press up and topstitch waistband near gathered seam line.

Attach apron ties here

Step # 6

Place apron ties onto protruding edges of waistband and stitch down. Finish off seam with a zigzag stitch or serging and then press ties out. Top stitch to reinforce ties to waistband.

Step # 7

Along stitching of hemline, sew a cloth measuring tape close to the edges of the tape. This keeps your measuring tape accessible at all times and will come in quite handy more than once!

" A stitch in time saves nine!"

Quilted Table Runner

Cut 4 squares that measure 12 ½" x 12 ½" from muslin cotton fabric. Choose 6 different printed cotton fabrics. Using about ¼ yard of each piece, cut the fabric into bias strips that are different widths. Choose widths from 1" - 2 ½" wide. Cutting strips in different widths will give you a pleasing design, rather than having them all the same width.

Take one of the muslin squares you cut and lay a bias strip, right side up, across the diagonal middle of the square. Baste or pin in place. Take a second bias strip of another fabric design and lay over the first strip, with the right sides together, and one raw edge of the strip even with each other. Use a scant ¼" seam allowance and sew along edge of strips, stitching through all three layers (muslin square, strip 1 and strip 2). Turn strip over to show the right side and press flat.

Place a bias strip of a 3rd choice of fabric, over the 2nd strip, right sides together and stitch as before through all the layers, including the muslin square.

Continue adding strips to your muslin square in this fashion, using the longer strips for the center areas and the shorter strips for the outer edges. Stitch on strips as directed above until your muslin square is covered. Press flat and trim around the outer edges to make strips even with the 12 ½" square. Continue doing this for the other 3 muslin squares.

Place 2 completed squares right sides together and stitch together using a scant ¼" seam on one edge. Do this with the other 2 squares until you have a long runner, about 4 feet long.

Take a remnant of co-ordinating or solid color fabric (you will need about ½ yard length) and place on back of your runner with wrong sides together. Press well and trim to the size of your runner of muslin pieced squares. Stitch with a long running stitch over the seams you formed with the bias strips in a random fashion, thus adding a quilted look to your runner.

Use purchased bias binding or cut strips 1" wide from a matchng fabric. They do not necessarily have to be cut on the bias since you will not be turning curves.

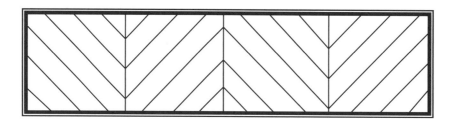

Piece these 1"-wide strips until you have enough to go all the way around your runner. Stitch this edging with right sides together and the raw edges of the runner and the strips even. Use a scant seam. Turn so right side of fabric shows and press well. Turn runner over to the back side and press over the edging strips and turn under raw edge and slip-stitch down.

You may use this table runner directly on the table or over a solid color tablecloth. If you have excess fabrics, you may cut cloth napkins to match. Standard napkin size is 16" x 16". Hem edges with a small rolled hem. ✑✑

Simple Curtains

Curtain panels or valances over a window add a homey touch when made from sheer lace . They are very simple to make. Take the measurement of your window. Cut your fabric 1 ½ to 2 x your window width. Use 2x the width for a fuller curtain. If your fabric is not wide enough, seam 2 widths together. Cut fabric to desired length of the curtain. You could cut it to be a short valance or make them half curtains or full length. You must remember to make an allowance and add for the fold overs for the curtain rod pocket and for the hem. (See diagram). Allow extra if you want a small ruffled header at the top of your rod. A 3" hem at the bottom edge looks nicer in a curtain than just a small, skimpy hem.

Press under allowance with a steam iron on both side edges (***) for hems (turning under the raw edge ¼") on the width of the fabric. Use 1" hems. Stitch down close to edge using a straight stitch on the machine.

Next, fold over the allowance (2") for a ruffled header and the rod pocket (2"). Press down and turn under raw edge and stitch. Stitch again 2" away from hemline stitching to make a rod pocket.

Hem across bottom edge, turning under raw edge ¼" and then turning up 4" allowance. Stitch down with a straight stitch. Press for crisp edges, slide rod into pocket. Slide onto curtain rods and hang rods.

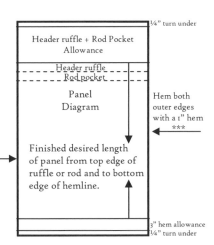

¼" turn under

Header ruffle + Rod Pocket Allowance

Header ruffle
Rod pocket

Panel
Diagram

Hem both
outer edges
with a 1" hem
***

Finished desired length
of panel from top edge of
ruffle or rod and to bottom
edge of hemline.

3" hem allowance
¼" turn under

Cloth Garment Hangers

Baste along outer edges of "TOP" ¼ inch away from raw edges. Pull basting thread to gather the stitches up to fit the "BOTTOM" piece. Pin in place and stitch with right sides together slightly inside the basting stitch line. Turn to right side.

Wrap the hanger hook with satin ribbon if desired. Take a small stitch to hold in place near the base of the hook or use a bit of fabric glue.

Cut 4 pieces of batting 8 inches wide by (hanger length divided by 2) + 3 inches. Wrap 2 layers of batting around each arm of hanger. Whip stitch to hold in place.

Slip covers over each arm of hanger and tuck in raw edges at the center. Slip stitch in tiny, neat stitches to hold the two arm covers together in the center. Tie satin ribbon around the neck of the hanger hook.

Contributed by ~ *Mrs. Sharon Castlebury*

❧ Pattern ❧

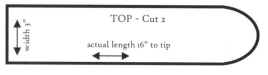

" *When you take them off. . .*
Hang them up!
When you hang them up . . .
Put them away!
That makes a nice end
to the close of this day! "

204

Cloth Napkins with Matching Table Cover

Cut a cardboard template that measures 17"x 17". Trace this onto your napkin fabric (cotton prints in medium weight fabric work best for not showing stains). Trace your pattern using a piece of colored chalk or a crayon. Cut inside traced line and hem on all 4 sides.

Lay a large piece of flat fabric on your table right side toward tabletop. (Flat bed sheets can be found inexpensively at discount or bargain stores and make lovely table covers!) With colored chalk, trace around your table edges onto the fabric. Remove fabric and measure down 9" from chalk line all around edges marking a new line. Cut on this newly marked line and then hem around the edges. If you want a longer drop, measure down from first chalk line by any amount of drop edge depth desired. Drop needs to be at least 6" to be a suitable table cover that hangs nicely over the edges. This method works well for oval or any other shape or size of table. If you are working with round tables you may need to add widths of fabric to each side of your fabric to make it wide enough to cover the table completely and have enough drop depth.

Easy Bed Comforter

Purchase a worn, but sturdy, bed comforter in the desired size from a thrift store. Cost is usually under $5.00. Launder using ¼ cup bleach in the wash water (no need to worry about color or spotting) and then dry thoroughly in fresh air and sunshine. Purchase 2 flat bed sheets in desired color or print. Cut to the size of the comforter leaving an extra 2 inches on the 2 side edges and the bottom end. Allow an extra 10 inches (longer than actual comforter size) at top edge of 1 piece; an extra 1 inch on the other. Fold down the top edge (towards the wrong side) of shorter piece 1 inch and then again 4 inches. This will make it shorter than the actual comforter. Press in place and pin down. Stitch down close to turned under edge. Fold down 2nd piece 2 inches towards wrong side and press in place and stitch down. Place the 2 pieces right sides together matching raw edges on 3 sides. Fold longer piece over 5 inches on top of shorter piece. Press down. Stitch along all 3 raw sides. Top edge will be a folded edge-do not stitch. Turn right side out and slide comforter inside as you would put a pillow into a pillowcase. Add Velcro™, buttons or snaps to keep top edge closed.

Drawstring Skirt

This is a very versatile skirt with a back pleat.
This skirt can be made of denim, soft cottons, or linen.

Getting Started

Enter your hip measurement [ ] + 3" = [ ] [W]

Enter your desired skirt length [ ] + 4" = [ ] [L]

Measure your waist to top of knee [ ] [K]

Drawstring ~ 2" x ([ ] [W] + 20") = [ ]

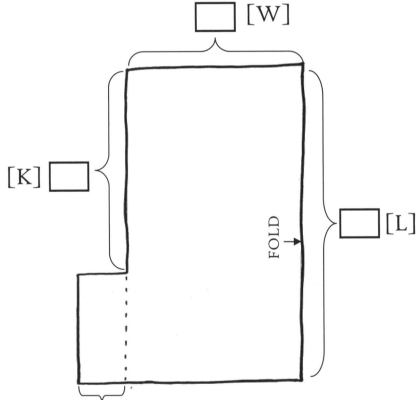

4" for knee-length skirt (pleat width)
7" for ankle-length skirt (pleat width)

Directions for Drawstring Skirt

1 ~ Zigzag waist edge and hem edge of skirt piece
2 ~ Stitch center back seam to [A]. Back stitch to secure.
3 ~ Stitch pleat extension. [B]
4 ~ Press up 2" for hem. Stitch. Open pleat. Press. Stitch top of pleat. [Fig.Z]
5 ~ Press under 1 ¼" to form waist band.
6 ~ Mark a button hole ½" on each side of center front ~ (to run a draw string out so it can be tied and adjusted to fit waistline.) [Fig.B] Each buttonhole is to be made ¾" long. Fold out the 1¼" pressed band. Make button holes.
7 ~ Prepare drawstring by pressing the 2 long edges together and stitching close to folded edges. [Fig.D]
8 ~ Fold down waistband and stitch very close to top of skirt waistband edge. Place center of drawstring under center back of waistband. [Fig.WB]
9 ~ Stitch from top of back center waistband, through drawstring, to edge of waistband, keeping drawstring flat, continue tucking drawstring inside waistband as you stitch the waistband down. (Be careful <u>not</u> to stitch through the drawstring again.) Slide one end of drawstring out the first buttonhole you come to, keeping the other end of the drawstring untwisted, slide it out the other buttonhole. Continue stitching all the way around waistband. Press all seams and wear!

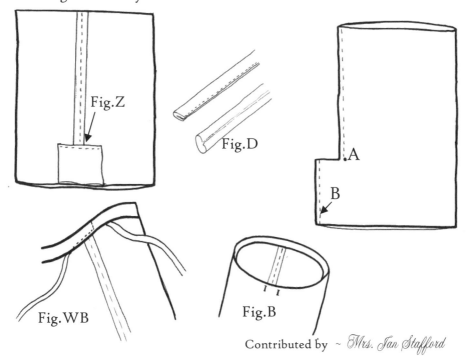

Fig.Z

Fig.D

A

B

Fig.WB

Fig.B

Contributed by ~ *Mrs. Jan Stafford*

207

Use this blank page for journaling or attach snippets and clippings for keepsakes.

Business
of the
Home

Use this blank page for journaling or attach snippets and clippings for keepsakes.

*"If your outgo exceeds your
income, then your upkeep will
be your downfall."*

211

Use this blank page for journaling or attach snippets and clippings for keepsakes.

Simple Home Repairs

Home repairs are the given responsibility of the man of the home. Many a homekeeper can take a little of the burden from her husband by keeping small things in good repair and taking care of the household that he has graciously provided. All it takes is a little creativity, some initiative, and a few simple tools.

Hang a shoe bag, with a cloth compartment of pockets, off the back of the door in your laundry room or all-purpose room. A closet in the hall would work well for placement of this bag, too. Keep essential items for small repairs and fix-its in the pockets. You will have the necessary items at your fingertips. Instead of purchasing a shoe bag, pocket compartments on a cloth backdrop can easily be made from scrap heavy weight fabrics such as old denim blue jeans.

Essential Items for a Handy Wife
small paintbrushes
W-D40™
extension cords
utility scissors
duct tape
hammer & screwdrivers
pliers
assorted nails and screws, hooks, and hardware
cloth rags
wood putty
all-purpose caulk & caulk gun
wood glue
glue gun and glue sticks
small bottle wood stain (for scratched furniture touch-ups)
utility razor and replacement blades

Each time a room in your home is given a fresh coat of paint, take a small 8 oz. glass bottle (or a small plastic, soda-pop bottle) and fill it with the leftover paint. Label the container with the room name and color information. Every time you see little scuffs and unsightly spots on your walls from furniture "bumps" or wear, clean the area with a damp cloth and allow to dry. Dab some of the paint from the appropriate bottle onto a cotton ball and rub gently over the spots. Your rooms will always have a look of being freshly painted!

If the grout around your bathtub or sink is unsightly and you know all the scrubbing in the world will not get it looking new, fill a small squirt bottle (you can use an old mustard squeeze bottle or empty dish detergent bottle) with chlorine bleach. Squirt around all the moldy, dirty grouted areas. Let stand for 15 minutes. Turn on the shower head or sink faucets and rinse it thoroughly. There is little need to scrub although an old toothbrush may be helpful around small cracks and areas around the faucets.

For chairs with cloth seats that are worn and faded: Give your home a fresh, new look. Buy fabric to co-ordinate with your room colors. These chairs are easy to recover and your only cost will be the fabric. Turn your chair upside down and remove the 4 screws in each corner. The seat will come loose. Lay this on a large piece of newspaper and draw a pattern from the seat. Give an extra easement to turn the fabric to the underside. Cut your newsprint pattern and measure to see how much fabric will be needed for your chairs. Cut each seat cover with extra edges allowed. Lay the seat cover on the center of the seat and stretch fabric over the edges. Secure down with small tacks or a heavy stapler. Replace the seat on the chair base and re-insert the screws. Turn your chair upright and you have a beautiful new–looking seat. You can just apply the new fabric over the old as it just adds extra padding.

To make nice drawer liners for the frequently used utensil drawers in your kitchen: Remove the drawer and cut a plastic placemat to fit inside the drawer. These are very durable and can easily be wiped clean. This is a nice repair for the inside of scratched, unsightly drawers.

If you have damaged concrete steps, or small cracks and holes that make them unsightly — here is a quick fix to make them look much better. Thoroughly wet the concrete stairs with a water hose. Sprinkle cement powder all over them in a thin layer. (Pure concrete powder, not a mix with sand or stone). Let it fill in all the cracks and holes. Then take an old broom and sweep your stairs until they are all covered nicely with a new coating of cement and the holes are filled. Allow it to dry slowly by giving the stairs a little mist of water a couple of times throughout the day, after you have swept them. Do NOT allow anyone to step on the stairs for 24 hours, to allow for a complete drying.

Use W-D40™ to eliminate squeaky doors and hinges.

Important Documents

Important documents should be kept in a secure location.
If kept in the home, they should be placed in a fire-proof
box with a small lock & key.
These would include:

DEEDS

TITLES to VEHICLES

TITLES to REAL ESTATE

LAST WILL & TESTAMENT

Record here a listing of your important documents and their locations.

Item	Location	File/Record Date

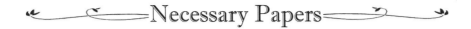

Necessary Papers

Certificates of Birth ~ A written statement by which the birth of a child is officially certified. It includes information on birthplace, date, and lineage. Originals should be kept in a secure location and photocopies kept in family files.

Graduation Diplomas ~ A certificate issued documenting completion of studies. These should be kept in a secure location for future reference.

Marriage Certificates ~ A certificate marking the date and witnesses of the bonds of holy matrimony, a legally binding relationship. This should be kept with the family files for documentation of the marriage relationship. It is also recorded at the courthouse in your locality.

Social Security Numbers ~ A number issued by the federal government of the United States of America to its citizens. Protected by privacy acts, it is used only in confidential transactions with a trusted establishment. It should be kept close at hand in a secure place for reference.

Important Numbers to Record:

_____ _____ _____
_____ _____ _____
_____ _____ _____
_____ _____ _____
_____ _____ _____
_____ _____ _____
_____ _____ _____
_____ _____ _____
_____ _____ _____

Home Inventory

This is important information. Record it here and then photocopy these pages and store the copies in a secure place such as a fire box or safe deposit box.

Bedrooms
Place a value amount by each item in [ ].

Bedding, linens, heirloom quilts, beds:

_____   _____
_____   _____
_____   _____
_____   _____
_____   _____
_____   _____
_____   _____
_____   _____

Furniture: Collectibles:

_____   _____
_____   _____
_____   _____
_____   _____
_____   _____
_____   _____

Contents of drawers ~ items of importance & value: (jewelry, etc.)

_____ _____ _____ _____
_____ _____ _____ _____
_____ _____ _____ _____
_____ _____ _____ _____
_____ _____ _____ _____
_____ _____ _____ _____

Rugs:

_____ _____ _____ _____
_____ _____ _____ _____

Electrical appliances:

_____ _____ _____ _____
_____ _____ _____ _____

Bathrooms
Place a value amount by each item in [ ].

Electrical appliances:

_____   _____
_____   _____
_____   _____
_____   _____

Linens:

_____   _____
_____   _____
_____   _____
_____   _____
_____   _____
_____   _____

Lamps:

_____ _____   _____ _____
_____ _____   _____ _____

Mirrors:

_____ _____   _____ _____
_____ _____   _____ _____

Basement ◊ Storage ◊ Garage
Place a value amount by each item in [ ]. Note serial or model #'s where applicable.

Hand tools:

_____   _____
_____   _____
_____   _____
_____   _____
_____   _____
_____   _____
_____   _____

Power tools:

_____   _____
_____   _____
_____   _____

Yard & garden tools:

_____ _____
_____ _____
_____ _____
_____ _____
_____ _____
_____ _____
_____ _____

Automobiles:

_____ _____
_____ _____
_____ _____

Washer & dryer:

_____ _____

Outdoor furniture:

_____ _____
_____ _____
_____ _____
_____ _____
_____ _____

Kitchen
Place a value amount by each item in [ ].

Appliances:

_____ _____
_____ _____
_____ _____

Furniture:

_____ _____
_____ _____
_____ _____

Kitchen, cont.

Utensils & Silver:

_____ _____
_____ _____
_____ _____
_____ _____
_____ _____
_____ _____
_____ _____
_____ _____

Kitchen equipment:

_____ _____
_____ _____
_____ _____

Dishes & china:

_____ _____
_____ _____
_____ _____
_____ _____
_____ _____

Note: Collectibles of any kind, furs, jewelry of value, and guns need to be thoroughly documented. It is also suggested by insurance companies that homeowners take photographs of everything in its normal setting and store this along with home inventory information in a firebox.

Living Room

Place a value amount by each item in [ ].

Lamps:

_____ _____
_____ _____

Paintings:

_____ _____
_____ _____
_____ _____
_____ _____

Furniture:

_____ _____
_____ _____
_____ _____
_____ _____
_____ _____
_____ _____

Curios:

_____ _____ _____ _____
_____ _____ _____ _____
_____ _____ _____ _____
_____ _____ _____ _____

Rugs:

_____ _____ _____ _____
_____ _____ _____ _____

Electrical appliances & electronic equipment:

_____ _____ _____ _____
_____ _____ _____ _____

Frugality

Economy in Expenses
Adapted from <u>Treatise on Domestic Economy</u>
by Catharine E. Beecher, 1841, Boston

It is impossible for a woman to practice a wise economy in expenditures,
unless she is taught how to do it by experiments in her life, or
by the special instructions of others who have had the experience.

Care needs to be taken to know these two things:
1 ~ Amount of Income
2 ~ Current Expenses

Expenditures must never exceed the means. Few women can do this
thoroughly or correctly unless a regular accounting is recorded.

Instructions on Recorded Accounts
Every evening before retiring, make an account of the day's expenses in
a small notebook. This procedure should take less than ten minutes of
your time. On each Saturday, take inventory of the stores at hand, of the
week's expenditures, and monies that came into the household. Record
exact expenditures and profits. After 2-3 weeks of this procedure, with a
little time devoted to this project, the homekeeper will know accurately
her income, expenditures, and profits. Make a list of your expenses for a
quarter of a year. Submit this list to your husband and ask for that
amount for your household budget.

Bank Information
Establishment:_____

Address:_____

Phone number:_____

Account Number:_____

Account Number:_____

Account Number:_____

"Little Problems of Married Life"
~ by William George Jordan

"There is one problem that dominates the home, an obtrusive, pervasive problem that ofttimes fills the whole horizon of life. It is the ever present question of home financing.

Saving means wise economy, careful planning, thoughtful management and prudent forethought in handling the home funds, be they large or small. If met in the proper spirit, it brings husband and wife into closer harmony, more loving cooperation and deeper recognition of mutual helpfulness. The wife, too, then becomes a money-earner, but it is in the sweet atmosphere of her home, where she belongs, she is practically earning money by her wise economy and her wise saving. The savings bank is the best and most practical way of keeping together small amounts of money, for it is safe, conservative, pays interest and is available when it becomes necessary to call on this reserve.

Systematic thrift will accomplish more than spurts and spasms of saving. If the members of the home finance committee decide they can afford to set aside monthly or weekly a regular stated sum from the family income, it should be reserved religiously, and this surplus should not be considered as really belonging to them but merely as a part of a little fortune they are preparing to come into at a later date. Saving does not imply penuriousness in the home life, but just wise watchfulness against invasion of the unnecessary, guarding against the little leakages of home expenses in proper harmony with the incoming funds. There are times when the needs of the home are so pressing and the income so small that it requires most careful straining merely to keep the ship afloat and saving seems impossible, but even here the true spirit of saving may serve to keep at the lowest possible point the creeping invasion of debt that must somehow be paid later. Debt becomes a hard mortgage to be paid off when times brighten, but it is a heavy, clogging burden easier to put on than to cast aside."

~ Excerpted from "THE DELINEATOR,"
1907, March Issue

223

Expense Record

Record a month of expenditures and incomes of your household here.
Keep a regular expense ledger of these and let it
become a habit to keep your ledger current.

MONTH of_____ in the YEAR of_____

Date	Income [+] Item & Amount	Date	Expense Item [-] & Amount

Your income must exceed your expenses!

Pages may be photocopied and kept in an expandable notebook.

MONTH of_____ in the YEAR of_____

Date	Income [+] Item & Amount	Date	Expense Item [-] & Amount
_____	_____	_____	_____
_____	_____	_____	_____
_____	_____	_____	_____
_____	_____	_____	_____
_____	_____	_____	_____
_____	_____	_____	_____
_____	_____	_____	_____
_____	_____	_____	_____
_____	_____	_____	_____
_____	_____	_____	_____
_____	_____	_____	_____
_____	_____	_____	_____
_____	_____	_____	_____
_____	_____	_____	_____
_____	_____	_____	_____
_____	_____	_____	_____
_____	_____	_____	_____
_____	_____	_____	_____
_____	_____	_____	_____
_____	_____	_____	_____
_____	_____	_____	_____
_____	_____	_____	_____
_____	_____	_____	_____
_____	_____	_____	_____
_____	_____	_____	_____

Use this blank page for journaling or attach snippets and clippings for keepsakes.

Family
Records

Use this blank page for journaling or attach snippets and clippings for keepsakes.

" The lines are fallen unto me in pleasant places;
yea, I have a goodly heritage."
Psalm 16:6

Use this blank page for journaling or attach snippets and clippings for keepsakes.

THIS CERTIFIES THAT

_____

and

_____

A E FOREMAN

WERE UNITED
IN THE

Sacred Union

of

Marriage

ON THE _____ DAY OF _____
IN THE YEAR OF OUR LORD

_____

AT _____ BY _____
WITNESS _____
WITNESS _____

" *What therefore God hath joined together,*
let not man put asunder.
Mark 10:3

231

Wife's Genealogy

Name

_____

Place photograph here

Brothers & Sisters

_____   _____

_____   _____

_____   _____

_____   _____

_____   _____

Mother _____

Grandmother

_____

Grandfather

_____

Father _____

Grandmother

_____

Grandfather

_____

Dated_____

Husband's Genealogy

Name

_____

Place
photograph
here

Brothers & Sisters

_____   _____
_____   _____
_____   _____
_____   _____
_____   _____

Mother _____

Grandmother

_____

Grandfather

_____

Father _____

Grandmother

_____

Grandfather

_____

Dated_____

Births

Given Name	Birthdate	Birthplace

Paste tiny footprint here.
Footprint form provided in the back of this album.
Remove or photocopy the form page.
Stamp footprint using an inked pad
on bordered form.
Press foot onto inked pad and carefully
press tiny foot onto paper.
Cut out with scissors around border and paste into this area.

"Lo, children are an heritage of the Lord:
and the fruit of the womb is his reward."
Psalm 127:3

234

Marriages

_____GIVEN TO_____
ON _____IN THE YEAR OF _____

_____GIVEN TO_____
ON _____IN THE YEAR OF _____

_____GIVEN TO_____
ON _____IN THE YEAR OF _____

_____GIVEN TO_____
ON _____IN THE YEAR OF _____

_____GIVEN TO_____
ON _____IN THE YEAR OF _____

_____GIVEN TO_____
ON _____IN THE YEAR OF _____

_____GIVEN TO_____
ON _____IN THE YEAR OF _____

_____GIVEN TO_____
ON _____IN THE YEAR OF _____

_____GIVEN TO_____
ON _____IN THE YEAR OF _____

_____GIVEN TO_____
ON _____IN THE YEAR OF _____

_"Wherefore they are no more twain, but one flesh. What therefore
God hath joined together, let not man put asunder."_
Matthew 19:6

235

Deaths

Name	Date	Burial Place

" Precious in the sight of the Lord is the death of his saints."
Psalm 116:15

The Family Crest

Make a link between the past and the present. Provide in the space below
some history of your family name or a drawing of your family crest.

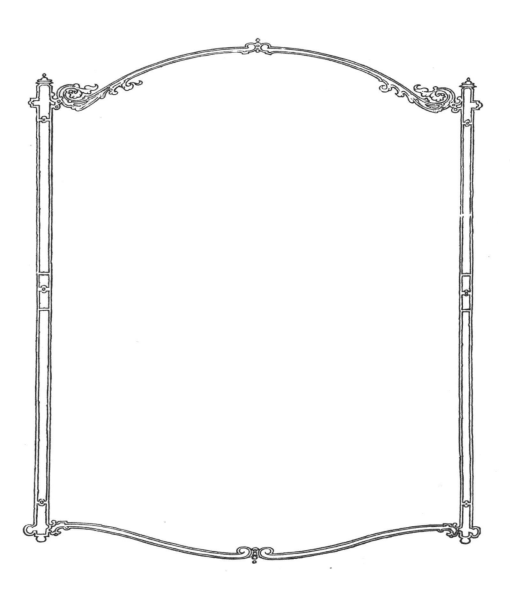

Resource
NAME HERITAGE INTERNATIONAL, LLC
12550 SW 16th Ave ~ Ocala, FL 34474 ~ 866.673.7455
Provides name histories, and genealogical searches along with family crests.

Our Family Creed

Compose a family creed and record it here.

_____

_____

_____

_____

_____

_____

_____

_____

_____

_____

_____

_____

_____

_____

_____

_____

_____

_____

_____

_____

_____

_____

Dated:_____

Family Creed ~ A brief statement of your family's persuasion, faith, and principles.

Our Family

Family portrait
pasted here

Home Sweet Home

Record descriptions and memories of home.

_____
_____
_____
_____
_____
_____
_____
_____
_____
_____
_____
_____
_____
_____
_____
_____
_____
_____
_____
_____
_____
_____
_____
_____

Footprint Form

Remove this page for use or photocopy to leave page intact.
Make foot imprint lengthwise. Let ink dry.
Cut around border outside line.
Paste onto page 234.

This form to be pasted on page 234 will
not give room for every child in the
family. Save it for a keepsake in this
treasury for the first child, last child or
the first grandchild. This treasury
could not contain the pages if it was an
all-inclusive album for your family.

"There is one vision that never fades from the soul,
And that is the vision of mother and of home.
No man in all his weary wanderings ever goes out
beyond the overshadowing arch of home.
Let him stand on the surf-beaten coast of the
Atlantic, or roam over western wilds and every
dash of the wave or murmur of the
breeze will whisper home, sweet home!"

~ from ~
Gathered Jewels for the Home Circle
S.C. Ferguson and E.A. Allen
~1882~

In the event of my death, I would like
for this Treasury to be passed to:

_____

_____

_____

Signed:

_____